MW00427585

PAUL'S LETTERS TO THE
THESSALONIANS
FREDERICK A. TATFORD

PAUL'S LETTERS TO THE
THESSALONIANS

FREDERICK A. TATFORD

LOIZEAUX BROTHERS
Neptune, New Jersey

JOHN RITCHIE LIMITED
Kilmarnock, Scotland

A publication of
Loizeaux Brothers, Inc.,
A Nonprofit Organization Devoted to the Lord's Work
and to the Spread of His Truth.

and

John Ritchie Limited

This commentary is based on the author's translation of
the Greek text of 1 and 2 Thessalonians.

ISBN: Loizeaux Brothers   0-87213-841-0
John Ritchie   0-946351-28-7

Library of Congress Cataloging-in-Publication Data

Tatford, Frederick A., 1901–
Paul's letters to the Thessalonians / Frederick A. Tatford.
p.   cm.
Includes bibliographical references.
ISBN 0-87213-841-0
1. Bible. N.T. Thessalonians–Commentaries.   I. Bible. N.T.
Thessalonians. English. Tatford. 1991   II. Title.
BS2725.3.T38   1991
227'.8106–dc20   90-48180

Printed in the United States of America.
10 9 8 7 6 5 4 3 2 1

To Harry and Judy

*(not forgetting
Daniel and Matthew)*

Contents

1

The Mission to Europe

The sailing boat glided along the quayside at Neapolis (or Kavalla as it is now called) to the mooring place. It had been a relatively short journey from Troas and they had sailed in the leeside of the islands most of the way. Before the cargo was discharged, a plank was thrown down for the few passengers to disembark. A group of four men, talking excitedly, was among the first to leave the ship. Their obvious leader was an unusual character. Although clearly a forceful personality, a now-ancient document said of him that he was "full of grace, for at times he looked like a man and at times he had the face of an angel" (*The Acts of Paul and Thecla*). A taller man, quiet and gentle, strode by his side, listening patiently to his friend's lively conversation, while two younger men followed, carrying knapsacks and small bags. One of the young men, clinging to his companion's arm, gave the impression of having a somewhat timid disposition. But the other, whose eyes darted hither and thither observing every detail, walked with the confident step of youthful assurance.

The port was evidently of no significance to them and, disdaining transport by horse or mule, the little party made their way on foot to the main highway, the Via Egnatia, which led them the nine miles to the Roman colony of Philippi. They were the first Christian missionaries to Europe, although this was the second missionary journey undertaken by

their leader, the apostle Paul. He had set out this time with his companion, Silvanus (or Silas), who had been a delegate from the Jerusalem
council, with the intention of evangelizing Asia Minor.

The two leaders had traveled through Syria and Cilicia and were joined
at Lystra by Timothy, who had been converted through the apostle Paul
and was therefore very devoted to the older man. They continued preaching through Phrygia and Galatia, but were not permitted by the Holy Spirit
to enter either Asia Minor or Bithynia. Instead, they were compelled
almost irresistibly to make their way to the Aegean coast, and eventually
arrived at Alexandrian Troas, where the young physician Luke joined
them.

As they faced the Hellespont, they had no conviction about their future
course. But that night a vision was given to Paul: a man was standing in
Macedonia and pleading with him, "Come over into Macedonia and help
us" (Acts 16:9). The party concluded that this was an indication of God's
will for them and accordingly they took a ship from Troas to Neapolis.

Philippi, to which they made their way from Neapolis, was an attractive
city, named after Philip of Macedon, which the Romans had converted
into a Roman colony and military settlement in 42 B.C. Eleven years later,
Augustus Caesar recolonized it and established an administration pat-
terned on that of Rome, with magistrates elected by the citizens, praetors,
and lictors. The Via Egnatia divided the city in two, the citadel and
temples to Silvanus and other deities being located in the upper part,
while the marketplace, forum, and courts of justice were found in the
lower part.

Paul and his companions spent some days at Philippi, where they
found a large company of Jews, who met in the open air—evidently
because a synagogue had not been established there. A number of Jews
and gentiles were converted through the preaching of the gospel, but it
was not long before difficulties arose. The missionaries' exorcism of a
demon-possessed girl, who was employed in a capacity akin to fortune-
telling, led to their being attacked, brutally treated, imprisoned, and later
being requested to leave the city. Paul, Sylvanus, and Timothy departed,
leaving Luke behind to care for the spiritual welfare of the new converts
and to guide them in forming a local church.

Once more the missionary band set out along the Via Egnatia for the
larger and more important city of Thessalonica, some ninety miles to the
west. The Via Egnatia, which ran from Dyrrachium on the Adriatic to
Byzantium (Constantinople) on the Bosphorus, and from there to Asia

Minor and the east, passed through Thessalonica and was virtually the city's main thoroughfare. Parts of it can still be seen. Trade poured into the city from east and west, and it enjoyed great prosperity under the Romans. Like others, the Roman statesman Cicero used to stay at Thessalonica en route to and from his province of Cilicia.

Thessalonica stood on the Thermaic Gulf (now the Gulf of Saloniki) and had an excellent harbor, which Xerxes made the naval base for his invasion of Europe. During the Roman period the dockyard was one of the finest in the world. It is still one of the principal ports of the Aegean.

Because of its hot springs the city was originally known as Therme. In 315 B.C., however, Cassander, one of Alexander the Great's generals, rebuilt it and forcibly populated it with the inhabitants of a number of villages in the area. He renamed it after his wife Thessalonica (Alexander's half-sister and a daughter of Philip of Macedon). After conquering Macedonia in 168 B.C., the Romans divided the kingdom into four districts and Thessalonica became the capital of one of these. In 146 B.C., when the four districts were once more united, the city became the capital of the united province. The Thessalonians sided with Augustus in the Roman civil war against Brutus and Cassius, and they were rewarded in 42 B.C. by being made a free city. The Roman proconsul of Macedonia had his official residence at Thessalonica, but had no control over the city's internal affairs; no Roman garrison was stationed there. It was governed by magistrates or politarchs, varying in number from five to seven, and had its own senate and public assembly. The citizens were proud of their status and sensitive to anything that might affect their political autonomy.

Thessalonica is still a prosperous city, well known for its tobacco, textiles, leather goods, and machine tools. It is also a beautiful city. G. G. Findlay wrote, in *The Epistles to the Thessalonians*: "It stands in a remarkably fine and picturesque situation, on a hill sloping down to the sea, and guarded by high mountain ridges on both sides. Below the city there stretched far to the southwest the broad and well-sheltered Thermaic Gulf (now the Gulf of Saloniki), with the snowy heights of Mount Olympus, the fabled home of the Greek gods, bounding the horizon" (10).

The ancient geographer Strabo declared that Thessalonica was the most populous city in Macedonia. At the time of the apostle Paul, the population was over 200,000; today it is at least 300,000. At the visit by the first missionary band, the inhabitants were mostly Greeks, although there were some Romans and Asians. A large community of Jews had established their own synagogue there.

The apostle Paul must have realized the evangelistic potential of this large and important city. If Christianity could be established here, not only was there the possibility of the entire province being affected through the capital, but the gospel could be carried east and west along the Via Egnatia and would conceivably reach Rome itself in due course and then spread throughout the empire. Paul's vision was never a restricted one. His strategy to present the claims of Christ to the whole world is evident from his New Testament letters.

So the missionary team (other than Luke) came to the capital of Macedonia and immediately made contact with the synagogue. Paul's practice, wherever possible, was to start preaching in the Jewish synagogues. There, as Roland Allen said in *Missionary Methods*, he found "an audience provided for him which understood the underlying principles of his religion, and was familiar with the texts on which he based his argument" (22). Here, using the Old Testament, Paul showed that the scriptures had predicted the death and resurrection of the messiah and then went on to affirm that Jesus was the messiah. They continued speaking in the synagogue for three sabbath days and it seems probable that opposition then forced them to preach elsewhere. But the record in Acts gives no exact information on this matter.

Some of the Jews evidently responded to the gospel preaching. Others attending the synagogue (described in Acts 17:4 as a great multitude of devout Greeks and not a few of the chief women), who may have been attracted by the purity and monotheism of Judaism in contrast to the immorality and many deities of the pagan religions, also displayed an interest in Paul's preaching. Evidently many of these also were converted. In *The Epistles of Paul to the Thessalonians*, W. Neil said of these Greek women, "This type of pagan—repelled by the laxity of conventional morality, unsatisfied by idol worship, and drawn by the high seriousness of the Jewish ethical code and the purity of its monotheism—proved to be the most fruitful ground for the activities of the Christian missionaries. Christianity offered them on a religious and moral plane what had attracted them to the synagogue, without the nationalistic bias, legalistic restrictions and ritual demands of Judaism" (xi). In addition, as the two epistles to the Thessalonians make clear, quite a number of people who had had no association with Judaism were converted from paganism (which supports the impression that the mission was not limited to the brief period in the synagogue). In *St. Paul the Traveller and the Roman Citizen*, Sir Wm. M. Ramsay argued that the missionaries must have labored in the city for at least six months in order to achieve the results that evidently accrued (228). Certainly they were there long enough to receive two gifts from Philippi (Philippians 4:16).

The success of the preaching aroused the opposition of the Jews, who had worked so hard to win proselytes to Judaism and now found them turning to Christianity. Eventually they gathered a crowd of troublemakers together and created no small commotion. They attacked the house of Jason, where the missionaries were residing, but could not locate their prey. Instead, they dragged Jason and others before the politarchs, charging them with leading a revolutionary movement and acting against imperial decrees by proclaiming "another king, one Jesus."

It was a serious charge, which might have had extremely unwelcome repercussions in the city. Paul had obviously referred to Christ's coming again as judge—and the one of whom he spoke had already been sentenced to death by a Roman judge on a charge of sedition. The politarchs were responsible to maintain the peace and to deal appropriately with any threats to Caesar. Since the offenders were not available, the politarchs took pledges of Jason and his friends that no further disturbances would arise from the preaching.

After that, it was impossible for Paul and his companions to remain in the city, so that night Paul and Silvanus escaped to Beroea, forty miles west and some distance south of the Via Egnatia. Whether Timothy accompanied them or followed soon afterward is not indicated in the Acts narrative. When the missionaries started preaching in the synagogue at Beroea, a number of people were converted there also. But the Jews who had been so embittered at Thessalonica stirred up fresh trouble at Beroea, and the Christians there conducted Paul to Athens, while Silvanus and Timothy carried on the work at Beroea. Although the apostle sent a request to his two companions to join him as soon as possible at Athens, it was some time before they were able to do so.

The apostle commenced preaching in the synagogue and marketplace at Athens, but the message did not receive as much response as previously. The climax was reached when the philosophers brought him to Areopagus, or Mars' Hill, and demanded an explanation of his teaching. He had toured the city and had seen the hundreds of altars and representations of pagan deities, but the altar that arrested his attention was one bearing the strange inscription, *Agnosto Theo* (To the Unknown God), and he immediately caught the attention of the Epicurean and Stoic philosophers by using that phrase as a starting point for his message.

Centuries earlier, Cylon and his followers had threatened the peace and security of Athens. The king, Megacles, offered complete amnesty if the rebels would submit, but when they accepted the royal pardon, Megacles revoked his promise and killed them. A plague ensued, which the Athenians attributed to the anger of one or more of the deities at the king's treachery. Although sacrifices were offered on the hundreds of altars in Athens, the plague continued. The poet-philosopher Epimendes of Crete was consulted and sacrifices were made to the unknown god who had thus to be appeased before the plague stopped.

Basing his address on the altar to the unknown god, the apostle Paul declared the god's true identity to be that of the Creator. Some turned to Christ as a result of Paul's preaching, but the general attitude led to his leaving Athens.

Before Paul departed, however, Timothy joined him. The apostle obviously welcomed the company of one of his co-workers, but his heart was with those in Thessalonica who had turned to Christ. He was anxious to know their spiritual state. Eventually his uncertainty about his "spiritual children" at Thessalonica overcame his desire for companionship and he sent Timothy back to see how they were. Had they been able to withstand persecution and tribulation?

The apostle moved on to Corinth where he spent eighteen months. Here, Silvanus rejoined him from Beroea and also Timothy from Thessalonica. The encouraging news brought by Timothy gave rise to the letters sent by Paul to the church at Thessalonica. Although there was an imperial postal system, it was not available for private correspondence. The apostle's letters were therefore carried to their destination either by a friend or by one of his co-workers, and it seems possible that Timothy himself may have been the courier. But of that, nothing is certain.

The date of both epistles sent by the apostle is generally assumed to be A.D. 50 or 51. That supposition is based on the date of Gallio's appointment as proconsul at Corinth in A.D. 51. On the other hand, it is not known how long Paul had been in Corinth when he was hauled before Gallio (Acts 18:12-16).

The two letters have been accepted as canonical from the second century. Their Pauline authorship was generally although not universally accepted until the nineteenth century, when F. C. Baur rejected it, but today no question is normally raised. Attacks made in the eighteenth century on authorship provided little argument currently worth consideration. Questions have sometimes been raised about the literary style and character of the presentation. W. Neil for example, wrote, "There is here none of the doctrinal finesse of Romans, or the logical dexterity of Galatians, or the mystic sublimities of Ephesians, but plain, almost disappointingly straightforward, normal letter-writing, with little of the vehemence and passion or, one might say, inspiration of the later and greater epistles" (xxvii). Nonetheless, little doubt can be cast on their authenticity.

Paul visited Macedonia once more on his third missionary journey (Acts 20:1-2) and doubtless spent some time at Thessalonica. This tends to be confirmed by the fact that two of the Thessalonian leaders, Aristarchus and Secundus, accompanied him on his subsequent journey to Jerusalem (Acts 20:4). Paul's last reference to Thessalonica was in his second letter to Timothy, "Demas has forsaken me, having loved the present age, and has gone to Thessalonica" (2 Timothy 4:10).

2

Correspondence with Friends

Whatever the length of time spent by the missionaries in Thessalonica—estimates vary from three weeks to six months—Paul's two letters to the Thessalonians suggest that the amount of teaching imparted to the new converts was significant. There had clearly been a ready ear for the truth. Itinerant preachers of many religions passed through the city and found a lucrative reward. Moreover, as W. L. Lane remarked in *Thessalonians*, "Stoic and Cynic philosophers grappled with the basic questions of life and ethics. Sophists of many schools proclaimed eloquently the way to wealth, fame and happiness." Only fifty miles to the southwest was Mount Olympus, fabled home of the gods, and the priests of paganism propounded their doctrines and claims without hindrance. J. B. Lightfoot in *Biblical Essays* stated that the cult of the Cabiri, a mystery religion second in popularity only to the Eleusinian Mysteries, was practiced in Thessalonica, with foul orgies (257). Temple prostitution was accepted as an integral part of the worship of certain deities and, in general, the sex-laden atmosphere was anything but conducive to spirituality.

When the Christian evangelistic campaign took place in A.D. 49, the effect on large numbers of people was equivalent to electric shock. The

16

biblical teaching with which it was accompanied was, for many former pagans, devastating but also enthralling. Apart from the moral instruction imparted, the revelation of the future—the detailed teaching on eschatology—had the effect of revolutionizing life and outlook.

But the wealth of knowledge thus made available also raised problems in the minds of adherents to the new faith. When Timothy returned to Corinth with the news for which Paul had waited so long, it was also with a number of questions to which he had been unable to provide the Thessalonian believers with satisfactory explanations. It was those concerns that gave rise to the apostle's letters to the young church.

The apostle's teaching about the second advent had had such profound effect on some of the Thessalonian Christians that they could think of little else. Some had abandoned working at their normal occupations in order to await the Lord's return with what has been described as "a kind of hysterical expectancy." It was necessary for that kind of behavior to be corrected, a further reason for Paul to write his letters. The ever-present temptation to revert to the immoral practices of paganism needed a reminder of the purity required of followers of Christ. In addition, a slanderous attack on the character and conduct of the apostle and his co-workers required rebuttal. There were ample reasons for Paul to write to his friends in Macedonia.

A. M. Harnack argued that, although the first epistle was sent to the entire church at Thessalonica, the second epistle was sent only to the Jewish Christians there, but it is difficult to sustain that view. Many points of similarity suggest that both letters were addressed to the same people. It has also been suggested by other critics that the second epistle was, in fact, the first to be written, and that the first epistle was actually the second to be sent, but that view is generally rejected today. There is little doubt that these letters were the first of Paul's epistles, and their character and contents are therefore of special interest.

G. G. Findlay claimed that "there is not a single quotation from the Old Testament in these epistles. St. Paul is addressing gentile converts, and in such a way that Scriptural proof and illustration are not required. But there are a number of evident allusions in that direction, showing how the writer's mind was coloured by the language of the Old Testament" (33-34). His comment is not entirely correct. To quote only one example, there is no doubt that, in 2 Thessalonians 2:8, the apostle was quoting Isaiah 11:4. In general, however, the Old Testament background, which would have appealed to the Jews, did not have the same significance for the gentile.

The following is a brief outline of the epistles.

First Epistle

1. Thanksgiving for the Thessalonians (1:1-10)
2. The apostle's conduct at Thessalonica (2:1-12)
3. Jewish persecution (2:13-16)
4. Paul's present attitude to the converts (2:17–3:13)
5. Christian morality (4:1-12)
6. The dead in Christ (4:13-18)
7. The sanctified life (5:1-28)

Second Epistle

1. Affliction and retribution (1:1-12)
2. The man of lawlessness (2:1-12)
3. Thanksgiving and prayer (2:13–3:5)
4. Discipline for the disorderly (3:6-18)

NOTE: The author has attempted in the following pages to arrive at the true meaning of the text by reference to a number of versions of the Bible and not merely to one of them.

3

The Fruit of the Gospel

1 Thessalonians 1:1-10

The epistles of Paul originally composed a single volume entitled *The Apostle*, the various letters being distinguished from each other by the names of the churches or persons to whom they were addressed. The Thessalonian epistles, although the earliest to be written, were usually placed toward the end of the collection, which was arranged in the presumed order of importance and not in chronological order. D. E. Hiebert rightly said in *The Thessalonian Epistles* that "the letters of Paul, characterized by a dynamic nature and permanent worth, are ageless treasures. Their enduring significance, their spiritual vitality, and their transforming power stamp these epistles as unique" (28). C. F. D. Moule observed, "There had been nothing quite like the Christian epistles previously—still less, before or since, has anything quite like the Pauline epistles appeared." They are still a challenge to the reader.

The Salutation

Paul, and Silvanus, and Timotheus, unto the church of the Thessalonians in God the Father and the Lord Jesus Christ: Grace to you, and peace, from God our Father, and the Lord Jesus Christ (1:1).

The apostle's practice was to dictate his letters to an amanuensis, but to add the closing lines in his own handwriting as authentication, and he did that in these two epistles. He followed the ordinary style of letter writing. W. Neil remarked, "A pagan letter, as has been established by the discoveries of papyri at Oxyrhynchus and elsewhere in Egypt, provided the pattern that we find more or less closely followed in all the Pauline letters: Greeting, Thanksgiving, Special Contents, Personal Messages, Salutation, and Farewell" (1).

It has been pointed out that the two letters are characterized by an "intensely personal nature. Most of the time, the apostle is not dealing with points of doctrine but with reminiscences of the mission, his own thoughts and prayers, and the small problems of congregational life. We are, therefore, given an insight into the nature of Paul the missionary such as we hardly get elsewhere."

The apostle's salutation conformed to the normal epistolary practice of the day. A letter would usually commence with the formula, "A to B, greeting," and Paul adopted that form for all his letters, although he varied the greetings somewhat. Here the greeting was conveyed in the names of Paul, Silvanus, and Timotheus.

Silas and Timothy had been Paul's companions at Thessalonica and the three were now together at Corinth. After the apostle left Corinth on his second missionary journey, they do not seem to have worked together again as a team. As was his custom, Paul included his two companions with him in the salutation, particularly as they had also been co-workers at Thessalonica and were known personally to those whom he was addressing. All three were Roman citizens, and Silas was also a leading member of the church at Jerusalem. Timothy, who had a Greek father and a Jewish mother, evidently acted as a youthful helper of the two older men.

Silas had been a representative of the church at Jerusalem to convey to the believers at Antioch the decisions of the Jerusalem council about the obligations of gentile converts. When Paul and Barnabas quarreled over John Mark, the apostle chose Silvanus to take the place of Barnabas (Acts 15:37-40).

The epistles were addressed "to the church of the Thessalonians," rather than in Paul's later style, "to the church at Thessalonica," but the reason for this slight difference is not obvious. He described the church as "in God the Father and the Lord Jesus Christ." The Thessalonian *ecclesia* was neither Jewish nor pagan, but Christian. As one writer remarked,

"Christians have a vital experiential relation in God the Father, who stands in opposition to the pagan gods they once served; their union with the Lord Jesus Christ sets them in contrast to the Christ-rejecting Jews."

The actual greeting was typically Pauline: "Grace to you, and peace, from God our Father, and the Lord Jesus Christ." The last nine words are omitted in some of the older manuscripts, but they appear again in the second epistle (2 Thessalonians 1:2) and there is little doubt that they are properly included in the first epistle. The usual greeting in Greek was *chairein* (joy) and in Hebrew *shalom* (peace). Paul used both in a deeper and more spiritual sense in his salutation: The grace of God has been manifested in Christ, who has become our peace.

Thanksgiving

We give thanks to God always for you all, making mention of you in our prayers; remembering without ceasing your work of faith, and labor of love, and patience of hope in our Lord Jesus Christ, before our God and Father (1:2-3).

The first chapter of the epistle represents a heartfelt outburst of thanksgiving on the part of the apostle at the report brought by Timothy concerning the Thessalonian believers and their personal and collective witness. His words were no formal expression, but the fervent and emphatic outpouring of gratitude to God for the conduct of those young converts. He naturally associated Silas and Timothy with him and declared that they constantly gave thanks to God for every one of the believers at Thessalonica. They were full of praise to the one who had so completely gained the loyalty and love of those who once served other gods.

There was, of course, no implication that the usual failings of Christians were not to be found in Thessalonica. But, as Hogg and Vine said in *The Epistles of Paul the Apostle to the Thessalonians*, "Christians differ in attainments, but there is always something of Christ in each, and hence always something for which to thank God."

Paul assured them also that, while the missionaries constantly gave thanks for the Thessalonian Christians, they also remembered them in their prayers—presumably the united prayers of the little band as well as their personal ones, indicating a fellowship in prayer as well as in preaching.

He then declared that the missionaries unceasingly recalled "before our God and Father" their "work of faith, and labor of love, and patience of hope in our Lord Jesus Christ." The cardinal virtues of Christianity were expressed in the most practical fashion and provided ample justification for the thanksgiving that had been expressed. One writer paraphrased 1:3: "How active and fruitful your faith has shown itself to be, how devoted and unwearied your love, and what fortitude your hope in the Lord Jesus has inspired."

In Thessalonica the devoted work was motivated by faith, the labor or exhausting toil was prompted by love, and the heroic endurance or patience was inspired by hope. J. B. Lightfoot said that "faith rests on the past, love works in the present, hope looks to the future." This is the first time in Paul's writings that work and faith are connected. The reference, as G. G. Findlay pointed out, "shows how far he was removed from antinomianism, from approving either a merely theoretical, or sentimental faith" (49).

All the activity of the believers (and not merely the hope, as suggested by some expositors) was "in our Lord Jesus Christ." All was undertaken by His enabling and enduement, and for His glory. The whole of the Christian life is directed to the honor of Christ. Life and its activities are all comprehended in Him. The Thessalonians lived as unto Him.

Election

Knowing, brethren beloved of God, your election (1:4).

The character and conduct of the Thessalonian believers were evidence of the reality of their relationship with God. As in the Ephesian letter (Ephesians 1:3-5), Paul recognized that their spiritual excellence was an indication of the divine choice of them. They were "beloved of God." The participle was not in the present tense, "as though the Thessalonians were simply loved now, in consequence of their newly acquired Christian worth; it is in the Greek perfect tense, signifying a love existing in the past and realized in the present, the antecedent and foundation of their goodness" (cf. 1 John 3:1).

The apostle, moreover, assured them of their *election*, which he declared that he and they knew. This is the first time in his epistles that reference is made to this important doctrine. Since he did not develop the subject here, it is evident that he had given clear instruction on it while in

Thessalonica. The substantive *ekloge* appears six times in the New Testament (Romans 9:11; 11:5,7,28; 1 Thessalonians 1:4; 2 Peter 1:10) and implies the choice of some from among others. Handley Moule said that it always "appears to denote an act of Divine selection taking effect upon human objects so as to bring them into special and saving relations with God." In the Old Testament, election applied particularly to the nation of Israel, but in the New Testament it relates to the choice of individuals for spiritual blessing.

God's supreme sovereignty and His rights are unchallengeable; as creator He has a perfect right to act as He decides in relation to human beings (Romans 9:20-24). At the same time, of course, His electing choice does not preclude human responsibility. Because of man's deliberate rebellion against God, he has forfeited all claim on his maker. Yet God, in a past eternity, planned the restoration of man to Himself and has predestined that we should be conformed to the image of Christ. He has provided the means of restoration through the work of Christ at Calvary, but the New Testament shows that there must be a personal human response (cf. Joshua 24:15).

Election is associated with God's foreknowledge (Romans 8:29-30; 1 Peter 1:2), but it is also clear that His choice is deliberate (John 6:37,44; Acts 13:48; Ephesians 1:4-5). The entire mass of humanity is under condemnation for its sin and rebellion. From that guilty mass God has chosen some to life. He does not elect to death and does not will that some should perish; His desire is that all should come to repentance (2 Peter 3:9). Those whom He has chosen have no ground for boasting, since it was a sovereign choice not based on the merit of the individual. Those who are lost have no complaint: they are already under condemnation and have no claim on God. They are already lost, fitted by their own sin for judgment (Romans 9:22). Divine election is preached to believers, however, and not to unbelievers. Leon Morris in *The Epistles of Paul to the Thessalonians* wrote, "It is not a device for sentencing men to eternal torment, but for rescuing them from it. Election protects us from thinking of salvation as depending on human whims, and roots it squarely in the will of God."

Findlay remarked, "Scripture does not speak of any choice of men to believe in Christ, but of the choice of (assumed) believers to receive salvation. The consistency of man's free will with God's sovereignty forms an insoluble mystery." W. Neil wrote, "Why God should choose one continent, one nation, one man rather than another is the unsolved mystery of the doctrine of election." That God is not arbitrary or unprincipled is clear from the revelation given of His holiness and justice.

The Gospel

For our gospel came not unto you in word only, but also in power, and in the Holy Spirit, and in much assurance; as you know what manner of men we were among you for your sake (1:5).

The evidence that the election was certain was afforded by the manner in which the gospel came to the Thessalonian believers. Paul referred to it as "our gospel." W. Neil pointed out: "It is now commonly accepted, firstly, that there was a common proclamation (*kerygma*) of the good news in the early church, and secondly, of what it consisted. This common *kerygma* is assumed in all of Paul's letters (see Acts 10:36-43; Romans 10:9; 1 Corinthians 11:23)" (15-16). It is perhaps significant that the apostle did not refer to the missionaries bringing the gospel to their hearers, but instead to the good news as revealing itself as an operative force through the messengers (cf. Romans 1:16).

Although the gospel was communicated to them in words, it came with a spiritual dynamic (*dynamos* or power). Behind the actual preaching a supernatural power was operating: the Holy Spirit was acting in the regeneration and transformation of those who listened. The AV adds "and in much assurance," but the RSV renders the phrase "and with full conviction," and the RV margin as "and much fullness" or "abundant fulfillment." The gospel had a complete effect on the hearers; the convicting power of the Holy Spirit completely fulfilled His purpose in them. Full assurance was theirs.

Paul appealed to the Thessalonians to recall the character of the missionaries while they were among the local church, to remember what manner of men they showed themselves to be. The message could not be dissociated from the messenger, and the character of the preachers clearly indicated the purity of their motivation. The work was not undertaken for the honor or benefit of the workers, but for the spiritual blessing of the converts. That was plain from their manner of life while serving the Lord in the city.

The Example

And you became imitators of us, and of the Lord, having received the word in much affliction, with joy of the Holy Spirit; so that you became an example to all who believe in Macedonia and Achaia (1:6-7).

The converts had perceived the effects of the gospel in the lives of those who preached to them, and the personal example had a natural effect on them. They became imitators of the preachers and commenced to pattern their lives on theirs. But Paul and his companions lived by the power of the indwelling Christ, and the character and integrity of their lives inevitably drew the hearts of their followers to the one who inspired them. Obviously Paul had set forth the glories and perfections of his master and, inescapably, the new converts were attracted, not merely to the servants, but to the Lord.

The reception of the word had involved the believers in "much affliction," or the most severe pressure. The word *thlipsis*, as Leon Morris pointed out, denotes "not mild discomfort, but great and sore difficulty." Christians in the primitive church always experienced suffering, affliction, and persecution, and that was especially the case at Thessalonica, where bitter controversy and strong opposition had occurred from the first preaching in the synagogue. To become a Christian inevitably brought trouble to an individual, not only the derision of the pagan but also the open violence of the Jew and the restraint of the civil authorities. But if these believers were suffering tribulation, they were simultaneously experiencing the compensatory joy with which the Holy Spirit flooded their beings.

The impact made by the faithfulness of the Thessalonian Christians was amazing. The apostle declared that they had become an example to all believers in their northern province of Macedonia (as Timothy must have confirmed on his return) as well as to those in the southern province of Achaia, where the missionary band was now temporarily located (at Corinth). It was a staggering statement, but there is no reason to assume, as many commentators do, that the apostle was indulging in hyperbole. The reputation of the Thessalonians had spread far and wide; they had become an example to all. The word *example* or *pattern* relates to a stamp made from a die. The implication is that, having been stamped

with the likeness of Christ, they became a stamp for the impression of the
same likeness on others.

A Living Testimony

*For from you has sounded out the word of the Lord, not only in
Macedonia and Achaia, but in every place your faith toward God
has gone forth, so that we have no need to say anything. For they
themselves report concerning us what manner of entering in we
had unto you; and how you turned to God from idols, to serve a
living and true God, and to wait for His Son from heaven, whom He
raised from the dead, Jesus, who delivers us from the wrath to
come (1:8-10).*

The apostle went on to develop the subject of their personal example, and
declared that the word of the Lord (i.e., not merely the gospel, but the full
declaration of the divine revelation) had sounded out from them like a
reverberating blast of a trumpet. It had reached not only the two provinces
of Macedonia and Achaia, he averred, but news of their faith had gone
forth "in every place" (cf. Psalm 19:4). The persecutions they were experiencing and their conduct in their tribulations served to advertise their
faith. Their conversion and subsequent experiences had created a sensation, the news of which was spreading beyond the limits of their own
country. No longer pagans or Jews, the entire tenor of their lives had
changed and was now directed godward. It was not an aggressive proclamation of the gospel which had that effect, but rather the news of the
complete change in their lives.

There was no need, therefore, for the missionaries to tell the story of
Thessalonica; the preparatory work for their ministry elsewhere had been
done by the reports being circulated. Those reports related what had
been done at Thessalonica and the remarkable consequences of the
preaching. Adam Clarke said that they were walking "so conscientiously
before God and man that their friends could speak of them without a
blush, and their adversaries could say nothing to their disgrace."

According to the reports, they had "turned to God from idols." Although some of the converts were apparently Jews or Jewish proselytes,
the majority were evidently gentiles and pagans, who had quite literally
turned their backs on paganism and idolatry to serve (literally as bondmen) the living and true God. They now acknowledged Him as the only

true God and placed themselves and their property at His disposal. They were bondmen to the supreme master. It was His character, His love and compassion, His saving power, that had attracted them and had nullified the appeal of the idols they had previously worshiped.

It is obvious from the two epistles that the apostle had taught a considerable amount about the Lord's coming and associated events. Naturally, therefore, he recorded that the believers were waiting for God's son from heaven. The hope of Christ's return characterized the primitive church. James Denney in *The Epistles to the Thessalonians* said, "That attitude of expectation is the bloom, as it were, of the Christian character. Without it there is something lacking; the Christian who does not look upward and onward wants [lacks] one mark of perfection." This hope affects one's entire attitude toward life and obviously featured large in the minds of those new Christians.

The one for whom they waited was the resurrected Christ, whom God had raised from the dead. It was the historical Jesus, who had lived on this earth, had died for man's sin, had been raised for man's justification, had ascended to heaven in token of God's acceptance of the sacrifice, and whose promise was that He would return. He was their deliverer from the wrath to come in the day of judgment.

For Christians, judgment is no threat and need present no fear. At Calvary, our substitute bore the penalty and has freed us forever from all fear of divine wrath. The Thessalonians could, therefore, rejoice that, for them, judgment was past. They owed everything to God's son.

F. F. Bruce in *1 and 2 Thessalonians* said, "The tendency of some modern exegetes to treat the wrath of God as an impersonal process of retribution operating in the universe does insufficient justice to Paul's thought. For Paul, God is personal, and his wrath must be as personal as his grace, even if his wrath be his 'strange work' (cf. Isaiah 28:21), in contrast to his proper and congenial work of justifying the ungodly (Romans 4:5)." From that wrath the believers at Thessalonica were delivered.

4

Apostolic Conduct

1 Thessalonians 2:1-16

After the enforced departure of the apostolic band from Thessalonica, their Jewish adversaries obviously conducted a campaign of slander and calumny against them, endeavoring to undermine the faith of the converts and their loyalty to Paul and his companions. Insinuations of insincere motives and charges of preaching for financial gain were leveled at the missionaries; it was evidently claimed that they were nothing more than religious charlatans. Doubts were instilled regarding their honesty and disinterestedness. It seems probable that others (possibly priests of the false gods) also were trying to discount the effects of the preaching by circulating false accusations and innuendoes. F. F. Bruce said, "So many wandering charlatans made their way about the Greek world, peddling their religious or philosophical nostrums, and living at the expense of their devotees, that it was necessary for Paul and his friends to emphasize the purity of their motives and actions by contrast with these" (26). The next section of the letter accordingly took the form of a defense against the calumnious statements.

Maltreatment

For you yourselves, brethren, know that our coming among you was not in vain, but having suffered before and been shamefully treated,

28

as you know, at Philippi, we took courage in our God to speak to you the gospel of God amid much conflict (2:1-2).

If others had questioned the value and motivation of the missionaries' work at Thessalonica, those to whom the apostle was writing could never have arrived at such a conclusion. They were aware from personal experience that the mission had not been void of substance and power. They, above all, must have realized the personal integrity and sincerity of the missionary band. Moreover, they knew how effective the message had been in their own lives. If Paul's honor and motives were impugned, they at least should have known how groundless those accusations were.

Refutation of such baseless attacks was essential, however distasteful self-defense must have been. So, the apostle recalled the experiences at Philippi. Although Paul and Silas were Roman citizens, they had suffered gross indignities, shameful treatment. Apprehended on an unsubstantiated charge, they were stripped of their clothes, publicly beaten without even a trial, and thrust into prison, their feet put in stocks as though they were dangerous malefactors. Such outrageous treatment of Roman citizens, which the magistrates at Philippi evidently hoped to cover up by releasing the prisoners and sending them away quietly (Acts 16:19-40), could have resulted in serious trouble for those responsible.

In spite of their experiences, however, the missionaries were spiritually emboldened to preach the gospel in Thessalonica. They were aware of the difficulties that might ensue and of the antagonism (following the Philippian pattern) they might anticipate, but they paid no regard to potential personal dangers. Again they boldly preached the gospel in the synagogue. Paul described it as "the gospel of God," indicating its origin and authorship.

They preached "amid much conflict," or against considerable opposition, as Acts 17:5-9 makes clear. It was scarcely the course that would be followed by men of the character now painted by their opponents.

The Preaching

For our exhortation was not of deceit, nor of uncleanness, nor in guile: but as we have been approved by God to be entrusted with the gospel, so we speak; not as pleasing men, but God who proves our hearts (2:3-4).

The apostolic defense turned to a complete repudiation of the slanderous statements made about the missionaries' motivation. A threefold attack had been made on what Paul termed "our exhortation," a phrase associated with the *paraclete* who is called alongside to help and which some versions have rendered by "appeal." Wm. Alexander explained that "as addressed to the careless, slothful, tempted, fallen, it is *exhortation*; as addressed to the sad and seeking, it is *solace* and *comfort*."

The first charge was that the apostolic message had sprung from deceit or, more appropriately, from error, in the sense that the missionaries had themselves been led astray in their concept of the message and had consequently led their converts astray. They had been deceived in their interpretation and representation. This the apostle rejected as untrue. They were not deceived; they did not deceive others; their message was not based on error or deceit.

Paul also repudiated the charge that their message was motivated by uncleanness (*akatharsia*). Although, as Findlay said, "This epithet commonly describes bodily defilement, and is a synonym for unchastity, as in chapter 4:7, etc. But there is a 'defilement of spirit' as well as 'of flesh' (2 Corinthians 7:1). Self-seeking (verse 5) in the witness of truth makes his testimony corrupt" (cf. 1 Timothy 6:5). The reference to an impure motive, therefore, probably relates to preaching for money or to secure prestige or honor.

On the other hand, Wm. Neil suggested that it "is a direct accusation of sexual immorality. Religious prostitution was very common in pagan temples, where it was justified on the grounds that union with a servant of the god was tantamount to union with the deity. Sacramental fornication was one of the foulest blots on pagan worship. . . . It was a favorite accusation of their opponents that the early Christians practiced sexual immorality. Some of their activities certainly gave color to this libel—such as the risky custom of encouraging unmarried men and women to live together as brother and sister (1 Corinthians 7:36ff), the ambiguous early name of the Lord's Supper which was the 'love feast,' the exchange of the kiss of peace, and the fact that in Rome at any rate the Christians met in the catacombs—a suitable place for nameless orgies" (37). It is questionable whether the apostle Paul was referring in 1 Corinthians 7:30ff to the early practice of believers of both sexes living in the same building. But, in any case, it is unlikely that the accusation made against the missionaries related to sexual immorality. It is much more probable that the reference was to impurity of motive in the preaching, and Paul, having maintained the truth of the message, now rebutted the suggestion of impure motives.

In addition, the slanderers alleged that the methods employed were directed to catching the unwary by guile. The apostle rejected that imputation also, and as Wm. Alexander said, denied that their preaching was "conceived and cradled, living and moving, in a congenial atmosphere of guile." Far from attempting to manipulate their hearers, the missionaries had been completely straightforward in their presentation of the message.

Paul declared that they had been approved by God to be entrusted with the gospel. They were not inexperienced novices, but men tried and proved by God for the work. G. Milligan in *St. Paul's Epistles to the Thessalonians* said that the term *approved* implied a fitness for election to public office. They had been tested in the local sphere before being called to the wider sphere of missionary service. The apostle audaciously implied that God was satisfied with them before entrusting them with the proclamation of the gospel on His behalf. Consequently, they spoke with the confidence and authority of those who had divinely received a particular assignment.

On the positive side, the apostle declared that their labors were not directed to pleasing men but God. No question of compromise could possibly arise. Their message was not shaped with the aim of securing a favorable reaction from their hearers. Rather, their loyalty was to God. Their only desire was to do His will and to bring honor to Him. They were always conscious that He was "proving their hearts" or testing their motives. Because there could be no deception of Him, their disclaimer of the accusation of unworthy motives was justified by the divine approval of which they were confident.

Flattery

For at no time did we resort to flattering words, as you know, nor a cloak of covetousness, as God is our witness: nor of men sought we glory, neither of you nor yet of others, when we might have been burdensome as apostles of Christ (2:5-6).

It was the consistent practice of the Lord's servants during their mission at Thessalonica to seek the good of their converts and to refrain from anything that might be attributed as a means to an end. They could, therefore, declare that at no time did they have recourse to flattery. As D. E. Hiebert said in *The Thessalonian Epistles*, "Flattery does not simply mean complimentary words intended pleasurably to tickle the ears of the hearers. It is rather the smooth-tongued discourse of the orator aimed at making a favorable impression in order to gain influence over others for selfish advantage" (89). The aim of flattery is almost always to secure an advantage for the flatterer. As the French fabulist La Fontaine expressed it, "Learn that every flatterer lives at the flattered listener's cost." That was not the way these Christian missionaries worked, and the apostle called on the memories of the Thessalonians to confirm his statement.

Many peripatetic preachers and philosophers of the day sought by every possible means to mulct their adherents, while concealing their personal aggrandizement. The opponents of the Christian missionary band had evidently insinuated that they were following a similar course. But Paul maintained that at no time had they been guilty of cupidity or avarice. They had never attempted to procure benefits for themselves under the cover of piety or devotion.

Paul called on God to witness that they had never used their preaching to obtain human approval or honor for themselves. They sought public esteem from no person, either from the Thessalonians or anyone else.

At the same time, the apostle intimated that as messengers of Christ they could justifiably have claimed recognition or "been burdensome" to their converts. Although they could have expected financial support, they had deliberately refused such a possibility in order that no criticism might arise.

Apostolic Consideration

But we were gentle among you as though a nurse was cherishing her own children: even so, yearning over you, we were well pleased to impart unto you not the gospel of God only, but also our own selves, because you became very dear to us (2:7-8).

Following his refutation of the charges made against him and his colleagues, Paul described in touching terms their actual conduct among the Thessalonians. In their ministry to the spiritual welfare of their converts, they exercised no dictatorial authority, but were gentle among them. (Most of the ancient authorities render the word *gentle* as "babes," this rendering depending on the repetition or omission of a single letter, but the AV reading suits the context better).

Their tenderness and care for the believers were evident to all, comparable to that of a nursing mother with her child at her breast. The term used for *cherish* was commonly employed of birds covering their young with their feathers to warm and protect them (cf. Numbers 11:12; Deuteronomy 22:6). F. F. Bruce quoted A. J. Malherbe as suggesting that the attitude alluded to here "forms a designed contrast to the harshness characteristic of one type of itinerant Cynic, who could not distinguish scurrilous reproach from admonition." The attitude of the Lord's messengers at Thessalonica should be a pattern for all Christian workers.

Their gracious and gentle behavior was expressed in a deep *yearning* over them that resembled a mother's love, "a term of endearment derived from the language of the nursery." The missionaries did not come to gain personal advantage from those who turned to them, but rather to share divine treasures—the gospel—with them. Further, they were willing to put their own lives in jeopardy for the sake of the converts (cf. Philippians 2:17). Because the sacrifice of themselves was not too great for the benefit of others, their ministry was characterized by an unstinting outpouring of emotion and affection.

A deep relationship developed between the converts and missionaries; the apostle declared that the believers at Thessalonica became very dear to the preachers. Throughout the apostle's correspondence, we see the strong affection he had for those whom he had led to Christ.

Self-Support

For you remember, brethren, our labor and travail, for working night and day that we might not lay a burden on any of you, we preached unto you the gospel of God. You are witnesses, and so is God, how holily and righteously and unblameably we behaved ourselves toward you that believe: as you know how we dealt with each of you, as a father with his own children, exhorting you and encouraging you, and testifying, in order that you should walk worthily of God, who calls you into His own kingdom and glory (2:9-12).

This final section of the apostle's defense again made an appeal to the Thessalonians' recollections. They were to remember how diligently the missionaries occupied themselves in the proclamation of the gospel and at the same time worked hard to support themselves in the material needs of life.

It was a traditional principle of Jewish rabbis that even a student of the law should be able to maintain himself by secular employment; a father was expected to make sure that his son had a trade or profession by which to support himself. Paul had been trained in tentmaking and frequently supported himself by so doing (cf. Acts 20:34). In this instance, he made no reference to the financial gifts received from the church at Philippi (Philippians 4:15-16), perhaps in order not to appear to be setting out a claim that a similar response should have been forthcoming at Thessalonica.

Many itinerant religious mountebanks consistently sought financial and material gifts. The apostolic band deliberately refrained from doing so. Rather, they preached the gospel at no expense to their hearers, refusing to be a burden to them in any way. The implication is not, as is sometimes suggested, that the Thessalonians were poor; the reverse is probably true. But, unlike the peripatetic philosophers who plundered their adherents, the missionaries were determined that there should be no trace of possible exploitation of the Christians by them.

In an unusual collocation of testimonies, Paul insisted that the Thessalonians and God also were witnesses to the behavior of the missionaries. They were free from a mercenary spirit. They displayed lives of piety, righteousness, and irreproachability. Their integrity, honesty, and uprightness could bear all scrutiny.

Succinctly, incisively, the apostle described the way they had dealt with their converts. The spiritual needs of each had been prayerfully assessed; the Lord's servants had concerned themselves with each one individually, showing love and consideration in caring for them. The shepherd's care they had displayed was comparable only to that of a father for his children.

By exhortation, encouragement, and testifying, they demonstrated their pastoral interest. Findlay said that "exhorting" is the general term for animating address; "encouraging," rendered uniformly in AV "comforting," is the calming and consoling side of exhortation, as addressed to the afflicted or the weak; "testifying" supplies its solemn, warning element. The Thessalonian church was both suffering and tempted, and the apostle's ministry to them had been both consolatory and admonitory. So are these two epistles.

The entire object of this ministry was that the believers should walk worthily of God, who was calling them into His kingdom and glory. To the Jew, the kingdom of God referred to the theocratic empire to be established on earth at the coming of the messiah, when all gentile power would be destroyed. But the apostle's words implied that the Thessalonian believers were already being brought by divine power into the kingdom of God and to an experience and appreciation of His glory. For them, the kingdom was not an earthly realm for which the planet still waits, but rather the spiritual sphere in which the rule of God is acknowledged as sole and supreme. The strongest possible incentive to holy living had been placed before these young converts; if they were called into God's kingdom, their character and conduct must be in accord with the divine mind and will. They must be holy as He is holy.

Further Thanksgiving

For this cause we also give thanks to God unceasingly that, when you received the word of God, which you heard from us, you accepted it not as the word of men, but as it is truly, the word of God, which also works effectually in you that believe (2:13).

It has been suggested that 2:13-16 is an interpolation, because of the repetition of thanksgiving, but the initial thanksgiving in 1:2 referred to the character and service of the Thessalonians. Here it related to their acceptance of the message. Paul constantly gave thanks to God for the reception accorded to the preaching. It had been received, he said, not merely as a message of human origin but in fact as it was: the word of God.

The hearers had spontaneously recognized the message as originating in God Himself; they had heard His voice through His servants. That was, of course, the primary purpose of preaching—that the purpose of God might be made known, that the divine voice might be made audible through human speech. Moreover, the word of God had operated effectually in them, bringing them not only to faith but also into subjection to the will of God.

Persecution

For you, brethren, became imitators of the churches of God in Christ Jesus which are in Judea, in that you also suffered the same things of your own countrymen, even as they did of the Jews, who both killed the Lord Jesus and their own prophets and drove us out, who do not please God and are opposed to all mankind, who forbid us to speak to the Gentiles that they may be saved; they always fill up the measure of their sins but wrath has overtaken them to an end (2:14-16).

Persecution had broken out early and the Thessalonian Christians had demonstrated the genuineness of their faith. They had followed the example of the churches in Judea, who had already experienced trial and tribulation. The Judean churches had been bitterly attacked by the Jews, and the Thessalonian believers were now being assailed by their own countrymen. The majority of the converts were gentiles, most won from paganism, although there were Jews and Jewish proselytes in the church. At the instigation of the priests of the pagan deities, the young church was constantly assailed and its members attacked. The hostility of compatriots was understandably a bitter ingredient in their sufferings.

The apostle, too, had suffered at the hands of his countrymen, and he declared quite bluntly that they had killed the Lord Jesus and the prophets. That was the accusation leveled at his murderers by Stephen at his martyrdom (Acts 7:52). They had killed many prophets in the past and, when the messiah appeared, they crucified Him.

They had driven out the missionaries from Thessalonica and had forbidden them to preach salvation to the gentiles. Their actions were not pleasing to God; they were an attempt to frustrate His purposes of blessing to others, and their rancor set them against all. Over a long period the Jews had been filling up the measure of their sins, like water dripping into a bucket. The implication here is that the measure was full. "Wrath has overtaken them to an end." They had decisively rejected the messiah and had refused to listen to the gospel preached by His servants. Now calamity was swiftly overtaking them. In A.D. 70, destruction fell on Jerusalem and judgment on the nation. A full account was required of them; wrath was now inescapable.

Paul was not suggesting, of course, that the retribution was a final and irrevocable rejection of all Jews; God still had His purposes for them. They were filling up the measure of their sins and, in due course, were to pay in full for their opposition to God. If the Thessalonians were suffering in similar fashion to their persecuted counterparts in Judea, their persecutors would also be dealt with in God's own time.

The apostle's denunciation of the Jewish adversaries has been described as a vitriolic polemic on the one hand, and as pardonable apostolic exasperation on the other. It may have been a vehement condemnation, but it was neither of the above. Rather, we read the words of a man inspired by God to indicate to the persecuted church at Thessalonica the principles on which God would deal with their persecutors.

5

Personal Separation

1 Thessalonians 2:17–3:13

T he next section of 1 Thessalonians (2:17–3:13) has been described as "the apostolic *parousia*" because "the apostle's authority is made effective in the church addressed as though he were actually present." It is, however, especially concerned with his absence from them and his desire to pay a further visit as soon as was practical.

A Hindered Visit

But we brethren, being bereft of you for a short time in presence, but not in heart, endeavoured the more exceedingly, with great longing, to see your face again. Therefore we had resolved to come to you, I, Paul, for my part, once and again, but Satan hindered us. For what is our hope, or joy, or crown of glorying? Are not even you in the presence of our Lord Jesus Christ at His coming? For you are our glory and joy (2:17-20).

After their enforced departure from the city, Paul felt like a father bereft of his children who ardently desired to see them again. The strong personal ties forged there demanded a renewal of personal contact. He had anticipated that the separation would be brief, but it had been prolonged more than could have been expected, and his desire to see the believers was consequently all the greater.

They may have been separated physically, but not in affection or love and, as time passed, the missionaries made every effort to return. They had resolved to come on at least two occasions, but Satan had hindered them. Whether the attitude of the Thessalonian politarchs or the opposition of the Jews or some other obstacle had prevented the visit is not clear, but Paul attributed it to the activity of Satan, the adversary. The scriptures reveal so much of the power of the devil that his influence and activity cannot be discounted; this example indicates that he is able at times even to thwart or frustrate the service of God's messengers.

If any of his calumniators perhaps questioned the apostle's long absence from his converts and the reality of his expressions of affection for them, he had a simple defense, asking rhetorically: "What is our hope, or joy, or crown of glorying? Are not even you in the presence of our Lord Jesus Christ at his coming? For you are our glory and joy."

Paul looked to the end. His hope was that his converts would not fail him or their Lord, but that their spiritual life would develop into maturity. His joy was in the fruit already borne in their lives and in the reward that would consequently be bestowed on them. His crown of glorying or boasting presumably had reference to the crown to be bestowed on him at the *bema*, or judgment seat of Christ, which was being fashioned in the converts he had won for his master.

Most expositors interpret the crown as the laurel wreath of the victor in the games (1 Corinthians 9:24-25). W. L. Lane linked it more closely with the Lord's return: "When a ruling monarch officially visited a Hellenistic city, the populace would form a triumphal procession to escort him into the city. Citizens knew when a state visit was planned because taxes were levied and contributions solicited in order to prepare an appropriate gift for the royal guest. A papyrus from the 3rd century B.C. speaks of contributions for a crown of gold to be presented to the king. While the monarchs of this world at their coming expect a costly crown, the Thessalonians themselves constitute the crown which Paul will joyfully present to Jesus at His coming."

The apostle here indicated that the Thessalonians formed the crown of the missionaries, referring to them as "our glory and crown." He linked the moment of supreme joy and exaltation with the *parousia* of the Lord

Jesus; that is, not His second advent in power and glory, but His presence among His own, when He descends to the air to receive them.

Timothy's Visit

Wherefore, when we could no longer forbear, we thought it good to be left behind alone at Athens, and sent Timothy, our brother and God's minister in the gospel of Christ, to establish you and to encourage you on behalf of the furtherance of your faith; that no one should be moved by these afflictions, for you yourselves know that hereunto we are appointed (3:1-3).

When Paul left Beroea, Silas and Timothy remained there. Timothy rejoined the apostle at Athens, and later both Silas and Timothy rejoined him at Corinth. The apostle evidently loved companionship, but his concern for the believers at Thessalonica far outweighed those personal considerations. Had the temptations of their former pagan worship proved too strong for any of them? What effect would persecution have on those who had so recently put their trust in Christ? Would they be able to withstand the antagonism of neighbors and the outright opposition of civil authorities? Would they succumb to the imperial demands for homage to be paid to Caesar?

Eventually he could bear it no longer and decided to send Timothy to Thessalonica to ascertain the spiritual welfare of the believers, even though it meant that he would be left alone in the unsympathetic city of Athens. He explained that, being unable to return himself, he had deemed it desirable for Timothy to come. He described the younger man very graciously as his brother and God's minister in the gospel of Christ. The AV renders it as "our brother and minister of God, and our fellowlabourer in the gospel of Christ," but the phrasing suggested above seems somewhat more accurate (cf. 1 Corinthians 3:9; 16:10; 2 Corinthians 6:1). Timothy was a servant of God in the propagation of the gospel and, by implication, was deserving of the respect of those to whom he was sent. The apostle's eulogy was obviously intended to secure that response for his emissary.

Apart from ascertaining the spiritual state and general condition of the church, Timothy's mission was twofold. First, he was to establish or strengthen the believers, to ensure their complete stability; he was to buttress their faith and confirm them in the truths they had been taught by the apostolic band. Second, he was to encourage them and fit them for the battle for their faith. Hiebert remarked: "Paul was well aware that a spectacular conversion was not enough; the converts also needed to be established and grounded in the faith. No small part of Paul's missionary labors were devoted to the establishing and strengthening of his converts (cf. Acts 15:32,41; 16:5; 18:23; Romans 1:11; 16:25). Paul felt that their premature separation from the Thessalonian converts had not given the missionaries sufficient time to establish and train them in their faith" (138). To do that, then, was to be Timothy's task. His work was for the sake of their faith.

A further purpose was that no one should be moved or perturbed by the afflictions or sufferings now confronting them. Such experiences were new to them and the apostle was concerned that some, agitated by the distresses, might waver in their faith. J. E. Frame suggested that the apostle had in mind not so much the persecutions which were arising, but rather the attempts by the heathen or by Jews to persuade the Christians to renounce their faith. He referred to "the cajoling insinuations of the Jews who would coax the converts away from the new faith on the pretense that persecution is evidence that the gospel which they welcomed is a delusion."

In his foresight the apostle attempted to guard against that possibility. "You yourselves know that hereunto we are appointed," he wrote. He had already warned them of this while he was with them (3:4). Suffering is part of the divine plan for the shaping of the individual Christian. Paul had expressed that plainly. "Through many tribulations we must enter into the kingdom of God" (Acts 14:22). Our Lord Himself had said, "In the world you will have tribulation" (John 16:33). Conversion does not secure immunity from trial and suffering; on the contrary, it ensures that that experience will come to the Christian.

Confirmation Sought

For truly, when we were with you, we used to tell you beforehand that we are to suffer affliction, even as it came to pass, as you know. For this cause, I also, when I could no longer forbear, sent that I might ascertain your faith, lest by any means the tempter should have tempted you, and our labour should be in vain (3:4-5).

The fact that affliction would be the lot of Christians should not have surprised the converts. Paul and his colleagues had explicitly taught, before the experience had come, that Christians were bound to suffer tribulation. As they now well knew, his words had proved true. Consternation was inappropriate. What they were experiencing was normal for believers.

Repeating what he had said earlier (3:1), Paul declared that it was because of his fears for them that he was impelled, when he could no longer bear the tension, to send for information about their spiritual condition, to discover whether they were still standing fast.

There was the apprehension that Satan the tempter might successfully have tempted them to forsake the faith, possibly by using the very troubles through which they were passing as an argument against their trust in Christ. This fear plainly wrung the apostle's heart and he felt compelled to discover the actual state of affairs. If the adversary's attempt to distract them from the faith had been successful, the labors of the missionary band had been in vain.

The apostle's fear was not an empty one. Many, possibly the majority, of the members of the church at Thessalonica had been won to Christ from heathenism. They had been worshipers of gods and goddesses all their lives; they had doubtless taken part in temple prostitution and fertility rites. The temptation to revert to their old faith was always present, and attempts to seduce them from Christ must have been frequent. Satan's emissaries were always available to assault the children of God and to lead them astray. Paul, well aware of the conditions, was justified in his anxiety.

Timothy's Report

But when Timothy came even now unto us from you, and brought us the good news of your faith and love, and that you have good remembrance of us always, longing to see us as we also to see you, for this cause, brethren, we were comforted about you in all our distress and affliction, through your faith. For now we live, if you stand fast in the Lord. What due return of thanksgiving can we make to God for you, for all the joy wherewith we rejoice on your account before our God? Night and day we pray beyond measure exceedingly that we may see your face and may perfect that which is lacking in your faith (3:6-10).

How long Timothy was away in Thessalonica is not indicated, but by the time he returned, Paul had moved on to Corinth. This letter was written immediately after Timothy's return (3:6). The report he brought was so encouraging that the apostle could not refrain from writing them at once. Timothy had come "even now unto us from you," he wrote. In spite of the persecution and troubles already being experienced, the good news of their faith and love (the former being their attitude to God, the latter their attitude to others) ended the apostle's suspense, filling his being with joy. That Paul was "a man of high-strung and ardent nature, sensitive in his affections to an extreme degree" is made clear in this paragraph.

If Paul constantly remembered the Thessalonian believers, he was now assured of the reciprocation of his feelings. They had "good remembrance . . . always" of him and his colleagues. He longed to see them, but their yearning was equally intense. Far from having any detrimental effect on their affection for him, when they heard the slanderous insinuations about the apostle their love was deeper than ever.

After the long period of anxiety, during which the apostle had suffered psychological distress and practical and physical difficulties (1 Corinthians 2:3), he had now been reassured by the news of their faith. "Now we live," he declared, or, more idiomatically, "Now life is worthwhile," since his beloved converts were standing fast in the Lord. The load of apprehension had been lifted; they were steadfast in the Lord, irrespective of their circumstances and trials. Although the words imply they must continue in that course, Paul seemed to have no doubt they would.

It was difficult for him to find words adequate to express his gratitude to God for what He had done in these new Christians. That they were steadfast and firm was not the result of the efforts of the missionaries but of the keeping power of God. What suitable return of thanksgiving could he possibly make to God for the abounding joy he felt at hearing about their conduct? His delight seemed to overflow at this report of these well-loved friends; inexpressible thanks were due to God for what He had done.

Paul prayed unceasingly for the possibility of reunion with them. Night and day he asked that he might once more see the Thessalonian Christians. There was nothing perfunctory about Paul's prayers; his petitions deserve study, both for their intense sincerity and for their spontaneity.

His desire was not only to see the converts once more, but also "to make good the deficiencies in" their faith. The time spent at Thessalonica had been insufficient to bring their faith and knowledge to full development. Now he longed to be able to impart what had not been given because of the missionaries' premature departure. Pastoral care and doctrinal instruction were still needed (cf. Ephesians 4:12).

Prayer

Now may our God and Father Himself and our Lord Jesus direct our way to you. And may the Lord make you to increase and abound in love to one another and to all, even as we also to you, to the end He may establish your hearts blameless in holiness before our God and Father at the coming of our Lord Jesus with all His saints (3:11-13).

The apostle's thanksgiving led him into specific prayer. Here, the way he addressed God has both grammatical and spiritual significance. The two titles *God* and *Father* are united under one article; *our Lord Jesus* is associated with God the Father. Bruce commented, "This close association of Christ with God the Father (cf. 1:1)—here, in His sharing the divine prerogative of directing the ways of men and women (cf. Psalm 32:8; 37:23; Proverbs 3:6; 16:9)—is theologically significant" (71). It is not irrelevant that the singular verb is employed.

Paul prayed first that God would direct his way to them or, more literally, make straight the way (meaning that the answer to his unceasing petition, already referred to in 3:10, might be granted). Second, he petitioned that the Lord would enlarge them and make them abound in love. The increase or enlargement did not relate primarily to an increase in their number, but to a fuller apprehension of God and of Christ and perhaps also of spiritual matters in general.

Abounding love would, of course, be a demonstration of their Christian character, and the apostolic prayer was not merely that such love should be shown to one another, but to all. In humility, Paul also prayed that his love to them might similarly abound. Although he had already disclosed his deep affection for them, he implied that there was still a wealth to be bestowed, but that enablement must come from God.

The object of such spiritual development was that they (or their hearts) might be firmly established blameless in holiness before their God and Father. The heart, as E. E. Hiebert noted, "is a comprehensive term standing for the whole inner life, including thought, feeling, and will." The heart is also regarded in scripture as the seat of one's intents and motives, and it is clearly in the sense of motivation that it is used here (3:13). The petition was that the inner sanctification effected by the operation of the Holy Spirit might be seen in blameless holiness before God. The apostle had already claimed that the missionaries had conducted themselves unblamably while in Thessalonica (2:10). Now he prayed for a fuller development of the same character in the believers. The resultant holiness would be manifested practically in every area of life.

The final clause in Greek is proleptic (anticipatory). They were to be thus approved of God "at the coming of our Lord Jesus with all His saints." The reference, of course, is to the *parousia* of Christ, His coming to the air (referred to again in chapter 4 of the epistle). It is then that the character of Christians will be made plain, when full manifestation comes at the judgment seat of Christ.

Because the coming is associated with "all His saints" (or "holy ones"), it has been claimed that the reference was to the event predicted in Zechariah 14:5, the coming of the messiah in power and glory. The angelic hosts who attend Him then will not be in evidence, however, at His coming for His church. But others will be brought with Him (4:14). It was doubtless to that event that the apostle referred. When He comes, every believer will meet Him, but not all will reveal the same degree of practical holiness as others.

6

Christian Morality

1 Thessalonians 4:1-12

Chapters 4 and 5 represent the second major division of the first epistle to the Thessalonians and deal primarily with practical exhortations, although 4:13 to 5:11 are concerned principally with the future. It has sometimes been suggested that these two chapters are a reply to questions posed by the Thessalonians in a letter, of which there is now no trace or, alternatively, to problems presented to Timothy on his visit and which he then relayed to Paul at Corinth. It is more probable that the topics arose from Timothy's report and his discussion with the apostle of the particular conditions at Thessalonica and the matters on which some guidance seemed desirable.

It is significant that the instruction about future events was both preceded and followed by sections concerning daily life and conduct. Today so often great interest is manifested in the details of prophecy, but the teaching seems to have little effect on the behavior of the hearers. (See 1 John 2:28 and 3:3.)

Behavior

For the rest, therefore, brethren, we beseech and exhort you in the Lord Jesus that, as you have received of us how you ought to walk

45

*and to please God, even as you do walk, that you abound more and
more. For you know what charges we gave you through the Lord
Jesus (4:1-2).*

The first three words mark a transition rather than a conclusion. Paul was
about to deal with practical matters of the Christian life. The Thessalonians had been taught by the missionary band not only the truths of the
gospel, but also the type of behavior that pleased God. Since they had
received instruction on Christian conduct, the apostle exhorted them in
the Lord Jesus (that is, as one member of Christ to another) so to conduct
themselves that they might please God, as well as, by implication, attest-
ing themselves to others.

The RV and other versions restore to the text the clause "even as you do
walk," which made it clear to those to whom Paul wrote that there was no
question of censure, but rather of a tactful appeal to continue in the same
way and to do so increasingly, to "abound more and more." His desire
was that their lives might be glorifying to Christ. Leon Morris commented:
"The Christian does not walk with a view to obtaining the maximum
amount of satisfaction for himself, but in order to please his Lord."

Instructions concerning particular details of conduct had been delivered by the evangelists with the authority of the Lord Jesus. Hence the
apostle referred to them as "charges" (cf. 1 Timothy 1:5,18). That refers
not only to advice publicly delivered, as Findlay suggested, but to commands issued with authority—used in the military sense of orders given
by a senior officer to a junior. Paul's readers would recall what had been
taught and be aware that the details which followed were not new instructions, but a restatement of what had already been voiced orally.

Sanctification

*For this is the will of God, even your sanctification, that you should
abstain from fornication; that each one of you should know how to
possess himself of his own vessel in sanctification and honour; not
in the passion of lust, like the Gentiles who know not God: that no
one transgress and take advantage of his brother in the matter;
because the Lord is an avenger in all these things, as we also
forewarned you and solemnly attested. For God has called us not
for uncleanness, but in sanctification. Therefore, he who rejects,
does not reject man but God who gives His Holy Spirit to you (4:3-8).*

It seems almost incredible that an injunction of this kind should have been necessary for Christians, but the words might well apply also to the twentieth century. It should be appreciated, as Wm. Barclay pointed out in *The Letters to Philippians, Colossians, and Thessalonians*, that these believers "had come from a society in which chastity was an unknown virtue; they were still in the midst of such a society, and the infection of it was playing upon them all the time . . . There never was an age in history when marriage vows were so disregarded and divorce so disastrously easy" (198).

The apostle, therefore, justifiably reminded his readers—as he must have taught them orally—that God's will was their sanctification, or their complete "setting apart" to Him. As far as their standing before God was concerned, they were sanctified to Him at the moment of conversion. In becoming members of the body of Christ, they were separated from the world and sanctified to God. Positionally, they could never be more sanctified than they were at that time.

But practical sanctification was another thing, and they were to demonstrate to the world that they had been separated to God, by the way in which they behaved in their daily lives. In the kind of society in which their lot was cast, purity of life and conduct was one of the outstanding indications of their relationship with Christ. Therefore, the apostle asserted that the will of God was their sanctification and went on to explain that this meant abstinence from fornication (cf. Acts 15:20,29).

The words were essential for, as W. L. Lane said, "In Hellenistic society generally, sexual morality was treated as a matter of relative indifference. Moreover, religious sanctions had become attached to forms of immorality, since fertility rites were an accepted form of consecration to the deity in certain of the mystery religions and cults. Believers needed careful and repeated instructions concerning the type of life which God demanded; specifically, that consecration to the living God was both religious and moral in character."

That must have been an entirely new concept to the Thessalonians when it was first enunciated by the evangelists, and it was consequently all the more essential to repeat it. The teaching was clear—that any sexual union outside marriage was forbidden. By marriage a husband and his wife became "one flesh." Union with anyone else destroyed that relationship and was therefore sinful. Yet, surrounding these Christians, there was the greatest possible license in sexual relationships. Demosthenes had declared, "We keep prostitutes for pleasure; we keep mistresses for the day-to-day needs of the body; we keep wives for the begetting of children and for the faithful guardianship of our homes." That kind of attitude was inappropriate for Christians.

The first injunction was abstinence from fornication. The second required the individual to know how to possess his own vessel. Each believer was responsible to understand how to act in this matter. There has been considerable argument about the interpretation of the word *vessel*—does 4:4-5 relate to the mastery of oneself or to one's personal relationship with one's wife?

The Christian who loses control of himself and becomes enslaved to sexual passion is no longer master of his body. If he desires to please God, he must maintain control of his body and his passions and allow the Spirit of God to sanctify body and desires.

Similarly, within the marriage union, the relationship should be in holiness and honor. Marriage is not a vehicle for licensed lust, as some seem to imagine. There must be regard for each other on the part of the two partners. As the apostle later indicated (1 Corinthians 7:3-5), there must be mutual realization that the two belong to each other; consequently, a denial of conjugal rights is inappropriate. And, inferentially, an abuse of conjugal rights is equally wrong.

Christian conduct in this area was not to follow the example of the gentiles, who had no knowledge of God and to whom lustful passion was a pattern of life. The apostle's words might well be taken to heart by Christians today. Moral laxity may be a principal contributor to the lack of blessing and spiritual power.

The third injunction is related to the potential wronging of another Christian in the matter of sexual relationships. The apostle's words were explicit: "that no one transgress and take advantage of his brother." It has sometimes been argued that 4:6 relates to enriching oneself at the expense of another Christian, or gaining some advantage over him, but the words "in the matter" obviously connect the subject with what has preceded. It is not a business deal or a legal process, but rather a question of adultery. The promiscuity common in Thessalonica might still affect an unsanctified believer and lead him into sexual relations with the wife of a fellow-believer.

Immorality is incompatible with allegiance to Christ. The apostle condemned it as totally unworthy of the believer. He recalled the admonition given while he was still with the Thessalonians. He had forewarned them and had solemnly attested that the Lord was an avenger in all which concerned a person's honor and the sacredness of the marital relationship. Violation of divine principles inevitably evoke divine judgment (Colossians 3:5-6). Faith in Christ demands a sanctified life and abstention from all impurity.

God called the Thessalonians to Himself, not that they might be free to continue in uncleanness and indulge in fleshly lust in the same ways as before their conversion. Their new call was "in sanctification"; the object was to separate from all that was sinful and defiling in order that a progressive holiness might be experienced in life.

The one who deliberately rejected the principles enunciated by the apostle in this matter—deeming the divine demand for purity of life as of so little importance that he could decline to obey it—was not rejecting the word of Paul and his colleagues, but rejecting God. How dare one flout God in such a fashion? It was He who bestowed the Holy Spirit on His people, and the mission of the Holy Spirit was to sanctify God's children to Him. For that purpose He took up residence in the body of a believer. For a person to indulge in sexual impurity was to dishonor the indwelling Spirit, as well as to repudiate the will of God Himself.

Sanctification is not restricted, of course, to the preservation of sexual purity. But the conditions in Thessalonica (and, to a great extent in the countries of the west today) required special concern in this area. In all spheres of life the injunction remains, "Be holy for I am holy."

Love and Industry

But as concerning brotherly love, you have no need for me to write to you, for you yourselves are taught of God to love one another. Indeed, you do it toward all the brethren who are in all Macedonia. But we exhort you, brethren, that you abound still more; and that you be ambitious to be quiet and to be occupied with your own affairs, and to work with your own hands, even as we charged you, so that you may conduct yourselves becomingly to those who are without, and may have need of nothing (4:9-12).

Turning from questions of morality and sexual purity, the apostle gave a further illustration of the effects of sanctification. Here was a subject on which he could unreservedly commend his readers. Learning of God, they demonstrated brotherly love for all who were members of the divine family. There was no need for any injunction, because they had displayed this love to all the believers in the entire province of Macedonia. Their recognition of their spiritual relationship and consequent responsibilities now evoked the apostle's commendation. Yet he urged them to abound still more in this Christian virtue.

Second, he exhorted them to be ambitious (or to labor) to be quiet. Here Findlay's comments deserve quoting in full: "The love of personal distinction was an active influence and potent for mischief in Greek city life; possibly the Thessalonians were touched with it, and betrayed symptoms of the restless and emulous spirit that afterward gave the apostle so much trouble at Corinth" (cf. 1 Timothy 2:2).

Ambition is a natural instinct, but its character and motivation need consideration. Thomas Wolsey justifiably counseled Henry VIII to "fling away ambition; by that sin fell the angels." In using the term the way he did, the apostle was saying, "Make it your ambition to have no ambition."

Paul used this term three times in his epistles (1 Thessalonians 4:11; Romans 15:20; 2 Corinthians 5:9). In the epistle to the Romans, he declared that he had made it his ambition to preach the gospel where Christ had not already been named, so that he did not build on another man's foundation. He was prepared to sacrifice everything in order to reach those who had never heard the gospel. To the Corinthians, he revealed that his ambition was to be accepted by Christ; he was concerned only with the master's final evaluation.

While the apostle urged the Thessalonians to be ambitious to lead a quiet life, unaffected by all the turmoil around them, he also urged them to attend to their own affairs. The true servant of Christ showed his character in his diligence and industriousness in business life. He did not meddle in the affairs of others but devoted himself to his own concerns— and presumptively those of his employer.

The third injunction—to labor with their own hands—implies that the majority of the members of the church were artisans, who practiced some handicraft. They were really being exhorted to expend their effort in the particular trade to which they were called. There may have been few wealthy people in the church; A. Plummer pointed out that the two epistles contain "no exhortations to the wealthy, and no warnings as to the deceitfulness of riches, although there was much wealth in Thessalonica." Paul had set the example there by working with his hands.

He reminded them that in all these things he had previously delivered a charge to them. The object of all his injunctions was that they might conduct themselves in a becoming manner among the unconverted and not attract criticism for unsuitable behavior. Also, by such conduct, they would be able to meet their material needs and have "need of nothing."

7

The Lord's Coming

1 Thessalonians 4:13-18

The apostle Paul frequently referred to the future, and particularly to the Lord's coming, in his letters. It seems clear that during the evangelistic campaign in Thessalonica the workers gave considerable instruction on future events and to no small extent drew on the Old Testament in their teaching. Anticipation of the Lord's coming had serious impact on the thinking and general attitude of the new converts. But in some instances it had resulted in considerable agitation and restlessness. Some individuals were thrown off balance and had given themselves to a life of idleness, arguing that the event was so imminent that activity of any kind was pointless. Others were evidently so excited that Paul's injunction to be ambitious to be quiet (4:11) was an essential one.

Problems had arisen that perplexed the church and then were posed to the apostle for solution. Whether or not they had misunderstood certain details of the instruction given by the missionary band or desired amplification of particular items, it was essential both to enlighten them further and to allay their fears.

The Dead in Christ

Now, brethren, we would not have you to be ignorant concerning those who have fallen asleep, in order that you may not sorrow,

51

*even as the rest who have no hope. For if we believe that Jesus died
and rose again, so also will God bring with Him those who have
fallen asleep through Jesus (4:13-14).*

Since the missionary band had left Thessalonica, death had taken its toll
on the little church. Some of the Christians had died, and the survivors
were naturally concerned about their future. Paul had described the glories of a coming day, when Christ would return to earth in power and glory
to establish the theocratic empire predicted by the Old Testament prophets. Paul had obviously taught them that, when Christ returned, He would
be accompanied by all His saints, and they would reign in association
with Him for a thousand years. Was that hope to be denied to those who
had already passed on? Were they to be deprived of participation in the
blessing and glory of the millennial reign? Some expositors assume that
the fear of the survivors was related to the Lord's coming to the air and the
possibility that their departed loved ones might not participate in the
"rapture."

It should be realized that, in general, the heathen world saw no future
beyond the grave. They met death in bleak hopelessness. Theocritus
suggested that "those who have died are without hope" and Catullus
stated that "when once our brief light sets, there is one perpetual night
through which we must sleep." Paganism, from which most of the Thessalonian Christians had come, offered no hope. It is little wonder that
confusion resulted as they argued and discussed the question.

On this matter, Paul wrote emphatically: "We do not wish you to be
ignorant," implying that he desired them to be fully aware and convinced
of the truth. His object was that they should not be overwhelmed by
sorrow or grief, like the rest of the people around them, who were without
hope. Findlay wrote, "Hopelessness was a prevalent feature of the world's
life at this time. The more enlightened and thoughtful a Greek or Roman
citizen might be, the less belief he commonly had in any existence beyond death. See, e.g., the speeches of Cato and of Caesar given in the
Catiline of Sallust" (101).

The apostle described the dead saints as having fallen asleep (a common euphemism among the Jews), the metaphor being suggested, of
course, by the stillness of the physical body at death. Another (and possibly more accurate) rendering is "those falling asleep from time to time."
The implication was not, of course, that the soul was in an unconscious
repose; the "sleep" had reference solely to the body. In *Issues of Life and
Death*, Sir Norman Anderson wrote, "When we die we pass out of a space-

time continuum into a realm where time is merged into eternity; so might it not be true that those who die in Christ are immediately with Him, in their resurrection bodies, at the Advent—which, while still future to those of us who still live in time, is to them already a present reality?" Anderson overlooks the chronological association of the bestowal of the resurrection bodies of those still living at the time of our Lord's return. He also ignores the implication of the Lord's words that the departed are conscious *now*.

Samuel was not sleeping when he was recalled to pronounce Saul's doom (1 Samuel 28:15). Moses and Elijah were not in unconscious oblivion when they spoke with their master on the mount of transfiguration (Luke 9:30-31). When our Lord, for a fleeting moment, drew aside the veil that hides the unseen, He disclosed that immediately after death (as bodiless spirits) we still retain our consciousness, memory, identity, personality, our capacity for sensation and recognition of others, our ability to think and speak (Luke 16:19-31). "Soul sleep" is not a biblical doctrine.

Paul then argued that "if [or since] we believe that Jesus died and rose again," there was obviously a prospect for the dead in Christ. If He died and rose again, surely those of His own who had died would also rise again. P. J. Gloag aptly wrote in *Thessalonians I, II—Expositions and Homiletics*, "The apostle's argument proceeds on the supposition that Christ and believers are one body, of which Christ is the head and believers are the members, and that consequently what happens to the head must happen to the members." The resurrection of Christ is the guarantee of the resurrection of His people.

The apostle referred to the Christian dead as having fallen asleep through Jesus. G. Smeaton in *The Apostle's Doctrine of the Atonement*, remarked, "Death is to the Christian no longer a penalty, but a falling asleep" (315). Again, it was through Jesus that this transformation had taken place and, as F. F. Bruce commented, "The continuing life of His people depends on, and is indeed an extension of His own risen life (cf. Romans 8:11; John 14:19)" (97).

There was no need for the unenlightened sorrow of the Thessalonians. Paul declared triumphantly that, when God brought back the risen Christ, He would also bring with Him those who had fallen asleep through Jesus. He was clearly not referring to their being brought back from the grave, since that subject is covered in 4:16. Rather, the implication is that they will be brought back with Him as members of His train. Some fifteen centuries ago John Chrysostom wrote, "When a king made his entrance into a city, certain ones among the dignitaries, the chief officials, and

those who were in the good graces of the sovereign, would go forth from
the city in order to meet Him, while the guilty and the criminals are kept
within the city where they await the sentences which the king will pronounce. In the same manner, when the Lord comes, the first group will go
forth to meet Him with assurance in the midst of the air, while the guilty
and those who are conscious of having committed many sins will await
below their judge."

If the apostle's reference to Christ's return (when God will bring the
sleeping saints with Him) related to His coming to earth in power and
glory, the question would immediately arise in the minds of Paul's readers: How could bodiless spirits be brought back to mingle with corporeal
human beings? If, on the other hand, he was referring to the coming to the
air to translate His people from earth to heaven, a similar question would
obviously arise regarding the mingling of spirits with living Christians
who still possessed their physical bodies. The verses that followed provided the explanation—namely, that the Christian dead would be the first
to receive their resurrection bodies.

The Rapture

*For this we say to you in a word of the Lord, that we who are alive,
who survive unto the coming of the Lord, shall in no wise precede
those who have fallen asleep. For the Lord himself will descend
from heaven with a shout of command, with the voice of an archangel, and with the trumpet of God. The dead in Christ will rise first.
Then we who are alive, who survive, will , together with them, be
caught up in clouds to meet the Lord in the air. So shall we be
forever with the Lord. Wherefore, comfort one another with these
words (4:15-18).*

It is significant that the apostle did not call on his readers to recollect
what had been taught them on the subject he was now discussing. The
implication is that either a new or a fuller revelation was being made,
evoked by the particular questions raised. Paul claimed divine authority
for the statement he was about to make. No recorded words of the master
threw light on this subject; the apostle may have been quoting one of the
agrapha (sayings of Christ), which has not been preserved in the canonical gospels (cf. Acts 20:35). But it is equally probable that a specific

revelation was made to him in order to meet this particular need. What he said was virtually a word from the Lord and therefore demanded the readers' full attention.

First of all, Paul made clear that, far from the dead in Christ being disadvantaged by the fact of their physical death, the living saints at Christ's coming would have no advantage whatsoever vis-a-vis those who had passed on. He described the living believers at that future moment in a dual fashion: (1) those who are alive and (2) those who survive unto the coming of the Lord, the second designation obviously qualifying the first. Inferentially, a generation of Christians will be alive at the time of the Lord's coming who will never experience physical death. Paul placed himself in that category by the use of the pronoun *we*. Later, even when early execution threatened him, he continued to express his hope of being alive at that time (e.g., 2 Corinthians 5:1-10; Philippians 1:21-24; 2 Timothy 4:8; Titus 2:11-13), although he also implied the possibility of having fallen asleep instead.

By no means would the living take precedence over those who had fallen asleep; they would certainly not meet the Lord before the believing dead had done so. As one writer remarked, "The shadow which the event of their premature death had cast over the fate of the sleeping Thessalonian believers was wholly imaginary, and should be dismissed at once from the minds of their sorrowing friends." This was plainly a revelation not previously made and was of utmost importance.

An explanation was obviously required and the apostle proceeded to disclose the details (evidently hitherto unrevealed). The Lord's coming would be with a military shout of command, such as a general might use in marshaling his forces, or a charioteer his horses.

That triumphant summoning shout would be with an archangel's voice. The implication was not that the shout would be accompanied by the voice of an archangel, but rather that it would be of that character and quality. Jude 9 refers to Michael as the archangel; no other member of the heavenly hierarchy is accorded that title, although Jewish tradition claims that there are seven chief angels. One tremendous shout of majesty and power would accomplish all that was required.

The trumpet of God would be heard simultaneously (cf. Psalm 47:5). The trumpet was commonly used in the nation of Israel in Old Testament days for the purpose of calling the people together or for directing their movement or advance (Numbers 10:1-10). This eschatological trumpet was clearly identical with that later referred to as "the last trumpet" in 1

Corinthians 15:52. In both cases the term is used in the context of Christians and the church. It is sometimes confused with the seventh trumpet
in Revelation 11:15, but that is associated with judgment and with the
"woe" that is to come upon the nations, whereas the trumpet in 1 Thessalonians 4:16 is related to the blessing of God's people.

At the stirring summons of our Lord, Paul declared that both dead and
living believers would be affected. First, the dead in Christ would rise.
There has been considerable argument as to whether the Old Testament
saints will be included in this resurrection from among the dead. But the
term used by the apostle was "the dead in Christ." In his epistles he
consistently used the expression "in Christ" in a semitechnical sense as
relating to members of the body of Christ, i.e., of the church. There are, of
course, stages in the first resurrection, but what was in view in this verse
was the resurrection of Christians who have died.

Speculation about the nature of the resurrection body is fruitless, since
the only indication given (applicable primarily to the living but also inferentially to the dead) is that it will be like our Lord's own body of glory
(Philippians 3:21). Dealing with the subject of resurrection in his first
Corinthian epistle, the apostle plainly indicated that although there would
obviously be some relationship, the body laid in the grave was not to be
identified completely with the future body, the latter being a body bestowed by God (1 Corinthians 15:37-38). The present body is dominated
by the soul; the resurrection body will be spiritual, or under the direction
of the spirit (1 Corinthians 15:44).

Only when the dead believers have received their resurrection bodies
will the living be affected. The apostle did not explain precisely what
would occur; later, in 1 Corinthians 15:53-54, he elaborated. The dead
who had suffered corruption would rise in incorruption, but the living
who were subject to mortality would "put on immortality." Both groups,
therefore, would be fitted for the presence of Christ (cf. 1 John 3:2) and
both would be caught up together to meet Him in the air. The verb
"caught up," as F. F. Bruce explained, "implies violent action, sometimes
indeed for the benefit of its object, as when the Roman soldiers snatched
Paul from the rioters in the Jerusalem council chamber (Acts 23:10)"
(102). By His tremendous power, our Lord will snatch away His people
from this planet, to be with Himself. The event is often referred to rather
appropriately as the "rapture" of the church, from the Latin word *rapturo*,
but that term is a nonbiblical one.

The explicit statement, that the happenings will occur "in a moment, in the twinkling of an eye," indicates that little will be realized by the world at the precise moment. The instantaneous disappearance of millions from all over the world simultaneously, however, is not an event that could pass entirely unnoticed. Whether it is correct to speak, as some do, of a "secret rapture" is open to doubt. It may be claimed that the shout and the trumpet are intended only for God's people and will be heard only by them, and it may therefore be argued that others will not be aware of what has happened until after the event. The question is not of great importance, since the effects of the event will become evident immediately afterward.

Hosts of people will be caught up together in clouds to meet the Lord in (or literally "into") the air. Our Lord departed from this world in a cloud, and the angels predicted that He would return in similar fashion (Acts 1:9-11). His return to earth as supreme sovereign will be "in a cloud with power and great glory" (Luke 21:27). When God descended at Sinai, it was in a thick cloud (Exodus 19:16). The rapture will occur in similar fashion; believers will be caught up into the air into clouds to meet their Lord there. The picture painted by some preachers of a cloud of believers traveling from the Antipodes, another from Africa, another from America, etc., is naturally appealing, but really irrelevant.

When that amazing event occurs, believers will henceforth "always be with the Lord" (John 12:26; 14:3). Whatever service lies ahead, whatever scenes of glory are to be experienced, and whatever the interrelationships of believers, those details find no place in the apostolic revelation to the Thessalonians. John may furnish some details in the apocalypse, but Paul was satisfied that the future was to be with Christ.

Logically, therefore, he enjoined the Thessalonians to comfort, or encourage, one another with the words he had just expressed. No longer need there be fear or doubt. Their loved ones were parted from them only temporarily. Soon the glad day of reunion would come.

Paul's words were recorded nearly two thousand years ago. Today the church is on the verge of entering into the presence of our Lord. In a very short while perhaps, He will come and every saint will be summoned to meet Him. We certainly ought to "encourage one another with these words." The hope of that event is the strongest possible incentive to sanctification of life (1 John 3:3), as well as to personal witness and service. No predicted event awaits fulfillment before our Lord's coming for His church. In the light of current trends and happenings, His return may occur in the very near future.

8

The Day of the Lord

1 Thessalonians 5:1-11

It is evident from both epistles to the Thessalonians that a considerable amount of oral teaching on eschatological subjects had taken place during the brief campaign in Thessalonica, and that the Christians there had no little understanding of the divine program. Evidently certain queries had arisen about details; it has been suggested by some writers that controversy over some points had occurred in the church. But there is no clear indication of this in these letters. Obviously, interest in prophecy was great and, in some instances, the effect of this had not been entirely commendable. Reproof had become essential. But Paul dealt sympathetically with the problems posed by the Thessalonians during Timothy's visit.

Having disposed of the problem of the departed believers in 4:13-18, he turned to another aspect of the endtimes in the first part of chapter 5. Many expositors regard 5:1-11 as the second half of a section commencing at 4:13, but the two subjects are not quite so intimately linked. In fact, the second epistle makes clear that the attempt to link them together had led to misunderstanding and had a detrimental effect on the character and conduct of some of the Thessalonians. A similar difficulty frequently arises today.

Times and Seasons

But concerning the times and seasons, brethren, you have no need that anything should be written to you. For yourselves know perfectly that the day of the Lord is coming as a thief in the night. For when they are saying, Peace and safety, then sudden destruction comes upon them, like birth-pangs on a woman with child, and they will in no wise escape (5:1-3).

Practically every student of prophecy is prone to a grave risk—namely, to try to determine the nature and chronological order of every detail of the prophetic program, as well as to look for signs that these events are about to occur. The Thessalonian Christians were not exempt from that risk. The apostle had given them a wealth of instruction, which must have included a great deal of detail, and evidently their curiosity had been stirred to desire even more understanding. Yet what had been imparted had led to controversy over the exact order and timing of future events.

Hence the apostle told them deliberately—and perhaps a little cynically—that they needed nothing to be written to them about times and seasons; they knew perfectly well the characteristics of the future day of judgment. The words used by the writer implied that his readers were aware of our Lord's own words prior to His ascension: "It is not for you to know the times or the seasons, which the Father has fixed by His own authority" (Acts 1:7). The words used related both to the duration of time (*chronoi*, times) and to the characteristics of a period of time (*kairoi*, seasons).

Paul's readers were, however, acquainted with the nature of the day of the Lord, the period during the time leading up to Christ's return to earth in power and glory to establish His millennial kingdom. The apostle's reasons for selecting this particular subject for further elucidation emerge more clearly in the second epistle, but some of them are evident in this chapter of the first epistle.

The expression "the day of the Lord" occurs repeatedly in the Old Testament prophets. There are nearly a hundred direct and indirect references to it, always in relation to judgment. Occasionally it is used metaphorically of an impending judgment for national transgressions or idolatry, but normally it relates to the final outpouring of divine wrath at the endtime. Isaiah, Joel, and others also disclose that the term covers an ultimate cataclysm involving heaven and earth (Isaiah 34:1-8; Joel 2:31).

It is the time when the Lord will break into human affairs to vindicate His righteousness and to execute judgment on sin and the sinner. Isaiah pictures the divine intervention as a storm sweeping over everything that man has exalted, bringing unmitigated wrath on a guilty world. Caves and holes will provide no possibility of eluding the terrible outpouring of divine vengeance. Not only human beings but inanimate nature also will come under the mighty hand of Jehovah, as E. J. Young said in *The Book of Isaiah* (vol. 1): "All nature is bound up with man in one common history; in every sense of the word this is a fallen creation, and because of man's sin, nature must suffer" (126).

A. B. Davidson wrote, "The day of the Lord is the moment when He grasps the reins which He seems to have held slackly before, when the currents of His moral rule, which had been running sluggishly, receive a mysterious quickening and the Lord's work upon the earth is at last fully performed." It should nevertheless be appreciated that God has never released the reins; He has never abdicated His sovereignty over the earth. Man has been permitted to choose his own way, frequently in rebellion against the supreme ruler, but the almighty has never vacated the throne. He has taken full note of the actions of His creatures, and eventually the accounting day must come.

The Old Testament describes the period as one of clouds and thick darkness (Ezekiel 30:1-3; Amos 5:18-20; Isaiah 13:10-11), of trembling and desolation (Isaiah 2:12; 13:9). Joel says that it is "a day of darkness and of gloominess, a day of clouds and of thick darkness" (Joel 2:2). Zephaniah refers to it as "a day of wrath, a day of trouble and distress, a day of wasteness and desolation, a day of darkness and gloominess, a day of clouds and thick darkness" when God declares, "I will bring distress upon men, that they shall walk like blind men, because they have sinned against the Lord" (Zephaniah 1:15-17). It is predominantly a period of divine wrath and vengeance (Isaiah 34:1,2,8; 61:2; 66:15-16; Jeremiah 46:10), when not only Israel but all nations will be affected (Joel 3:12-14; Obadiah 15; Zechariah 14:1-3). The New Testament makes it clear that it will come unexpectedly, like a thief in the night (Luke 21:34-35; 1 Thessalonians 5:2; 2 Peter 3:10).

The apostle made clear in 2 Thessalonians that the day of the Lord was still future at that time and that it would not commence until the appearance of the "man of lawlessness." Matthew 24:15 and Mark 13:14 imply that that event will occur halfway through the last period of seven years in Daniel 9:27, i.e., at least three-and-a-half years after the removal of the church. Second Peter 3:10-13 shows that the period will continue until the dissolution of the earth after the final rebellion at the end of the millennium (Revelation 20:7-9). The day of the Lord is, therefore, a long period of judgment running from the commencement of the great tribulation to the end of time, the millennial reign of Christ being a long parenthetical age of blessing interposed before the final outpouring of judgment and the introduction of the eternal state.

Like Peter, the apostle Paul declared that the day of the Lord would come suddenly and unexpectedly, "as a thief in the night." The thief steals in, stealthily and surreptitiously at dead of night, when the householder is asleep and when burglary is not expected. So will it be at the coming of the day of the Lord. The world will be boasting of safety and security and there will be no anticipation of trouble. But at that moment, sudden destruction will come, just like the travail or birth pangs of a pregnant woman. And, Paul added in solemn terms, "they will in no wise escape." When the hand of God falls in judgment, none can possibly avoid it. Those concerned may have been congratulating themselves on the stability and security of the world at that time, but their doom is inevitable.

Children of Light

But you, brethren, are not in darkness, that that day should overtake you as a thief. For you are all sons of light and sons of day: we are not of the night, nor of darkness. So then, let us not sleep, as do others, but let us keep awake and be sober. For those who sleep sleep in the night, and those who are drunk are drunk in the night (5:4-7).

The unregenerate were in spiritual darkness and consequently were oblivious to the danger and judgment impending. By contrast, the believers had been spiritually enlightened and were no longer in the darkness of ignorance and unbelief. While unbelievers would be overtaken by the destruction, which was to come on all who were estranged from God, it would be different for the believers.

Paul declared that they were all sons of light (cf. Luke 16:8; Ephesians 5:8) and sons of day (Romans 13:12). Findlay said, "By a common Hebrew idiom, a man is said to be a son of any influence that determines or dominates his character. So there are 'sons of Belial' (worthlessness) in the O. T., and Christ speaks of 'sons of thunder,' 'sons of resurrection,' etc." Christians have nothing to do with the day of the Lord, but they do enjoy the glorious sunshine of the day of Christ. Our Lord declared that He was "the light of the world" (John 8:12), but He also told His followers, "You are the light of the world" (Matthew 5:14). His people belong to the day and to the light. Then the apostle Paul passed from the second person to the first and maintained, "We are not of the night nor of darkness." Since believers have been translated from the kingdom of darkness into the kingdom of God's son (Colossians 1:13), the judgment of the day of the Lord has nothing to do with them.

Accordingly, there was a practical responsibility. The insensibility and indifference of the unbelieving world allowed them to lapse into sleep. "Let us not sleep, as do others" (or "the rest"), the apostle enjoined. To succumb to sloth and lethargy is not for the Christian. "Let us keep awake and be sober." There was the constant need for alertness against the surrounding evil, against the assaults of the devil, but vigilance was to be accompanied by sobriety (Romans 13:11-14). The reference was not merely to abstinence from intoxication, but to complete freedom from the stupefying effects of sin, the world, and self-indulgence. The injunction is still relevant.

Vigilance and sobriety are imperative for children of light. Those who are children of darkness are of a totally different character. The sleeper sleeps at night and the drunkard satisfies his desire for drink at night. Drunkenness in the daytime was regarded as disgraceful (cf. Acts 2:15). The besotted individual gives way to wantonness at night; when the dawn surprises the guilty revelers, its is considered a shame. Sleep and drunkenness, in Paul's view, characterize the children of the night, but watchfulness and sobriety are features of the children of the day.

The Christian Armor

But let us, since we are of the day, be sober, putting on the breastplate of faith and love: and for a helmet the hope of salvation. Because God has not appointed us to wrath, but to the obtaining of salvation through our Lord Jesus Christ, who died for us so that, whether we are awake or asleep, we might live together with Him. Wherefore, encourage one another and build each other up, even as also you do (5:8-11).

A. T. Robertson said that "the idea of watchfulness brings the figure of a sentry, on guard and armed, to Paul's mind," and he naturally employed that symbolism. Since his readers belonged to the day, he reiterated that they should be sober. Like a sentry, they should don breastplate and helmet to protect them in the strife (cf. Isaiah 59:17; Ephesians 6:11-18). The breastplate was double, its two sides covering the wearer's front and back. It covered him from neck to waist and thus protected the heart and the most vulnerable parts of the body. John Trapp remarked that "Faith is the fore-part of this breastplate, whereby we embrace Christ, and love the hinder part thereof, whereby we embosom the saints." The helmet covered the head, and was described by Paul as "the hope of salvation," so that the Christian armor was also associated with the three cardinal virtues of Christianity: faith, love, and hope. The head needed protection since it was the part of the body most severely attacked.

The mention of salvation immediately directed the apostle's thoughts to all the blessings that had accrued to the believer through the work of Christ. Paul declared triumphantly that God had not appointed the Christian to wrath. Presumably the statement had a dual significance. The believer had been delivered from the day of judgment, the day of the Lord, which he had been explaining to his readers. But it was, of course, equally true that he had been delivered from the ultimate judgment at the great white throne.

God's purpose for the believer was that he might obtain salvation—total deliverance from the wrath of God—through the Lord Jesus Christ. There was no doubt about the source or channel. Salvation was acquired by the Christian solely through the work of Christ. The Savior died for him and thereby guaranteed his security. Christ's death and resurrection were, moreover, the pledge that the believer would live together with the Savior. Whether the Christian was awake or asleep, alive or dead, made no difference to the ultimate prospect.

In view of the apostle's earlier references to watching and sleeping, it is possible that his words also covered a question current today, even if not in the Thessalonian church. It is argued by some that the New Testament's many injunctions to watch have a connotation of loss if the individual fails to watch. In that view, only those who are watching and waiting will be caught up to meet the Lord when He descends into the air. The carnal Christian, who is not watching and waiting, will, it is said, be left behind for a period of trial (verging, according to some teachers, on something like purgatory). In other words, the rapture of the believer depends on his fidelity in life.

The salvation of the individual is not dependent on his or her morality or personal righteousness; it results solely from the grace of God revealed in the work of Christ at Calvary. Christians have not "kept themselves" during their earthly pilgrimage; they have been kept by the power of God. Their rapture at the coming of Christ does not depend on them but on Christ. Our Lord will return to take to glory His mystical body, the church. He will certainly not take an incomplete or mutilated body. The case might be argued at length, but a brief examination of the New Testament teaching should convince an unbiased reader that the theory of a partial rapture really has no scriptural support and is therefore untenable.

Having regard to all he had written, the apostle not unnaturally urged the Thessalonians to encourage and build up one another, acknowledging that they already were doing this—as was evident from Timothy's report.

9

Relationships and Conduct

1 Thessalonians 5:12-28

T he apostle had dealt with the major problems that the Thessalonian Christians had presented to Timothy and had emphasized the hope of Christ's coming as the mainspring of life. As F. F. Bruce remarked, "Plainly the Advent hope is treated as an incentive to Christian life and conduct here and now. The motive power for Christian life and conduct is supplied by the indwelling Spirit (cf. 4:8); it is His indwelling presence, indeed as other letters of Paul make plain, that ensures that the Advent hope is no vain hope but one which, because it is so well founded, is ethically fruitful in the present mortal existence" (116).

Christ is at our doors. This fact provides strong incentive to Christian living today.

It was logical that the apostle should devote the remainder of the first epistle to a series of injunctions and exhortations about Christian conduct, a valuable section of the epistle.

Attitude to Elders

Now we beseech you, brethren, to know those who labour among you and are over you in the Lord and admonish you, and to esteem them very highly in love because of their work (5:12-13a).

This new section is introduced in a solicitous manner, as an appeal to brothers rather than as an authoritative instruction on conduct. There is possibly a hint of some deficiency in the church or perhaps of some personal difficulty in connection with the matter of eldership. The introductory words are certainly indicative of the apostle's gentle tact. Although he might have claimed the right to give directions in ecclesiastical matters because of his experience in church planting and his special relationship with Thessalonica as spiritual father of the believers, he disregarded any authority he might have been deemed to possess, and besought his brothers in Christ to adopt particular attitudes.

Although recognizing the sufficiency of the Holy Spirit in guiding the local church, it was the practice of the apostle and his colleagues to appoint elders wherever suitably qualified men had proved their ability (Acts 14:23; Titus 1:5). He later set out the qualifications of elders and deacons (1 Timothy 3:1-12; Titus 1:5-9). W. L. Lane suggested that the elders at Thessalonica included Jason (Acts 17:5), Secundus (Acts 20:4), and Demas (2 Timothy 4:10), but there is no real evidence of this. It is clear that elders (and doubtless deacons also) had been appointed at Thessalonica since Paul here enjoined their recognition and exhorted his readers to pay them the highest respect for their work.

F. F. Bruce commented, "No fixed pattern of rule appears to have been imposed on the Pauline churches. The precedent of the church at Jerusalem, which by this time was governed by a body of elders under the chairmanship of James the Just, was not followed as a matter of course. The policy of Paul and his colleagues seems to have been to wait until qualities of spiritual leadership displayed themselves in certain members of a church and then to urge the others to acknowledge and respect those as leaders. One of the most obvious qualities of leadership was a readiness to serve the church and care for its needs. Such leaders did not do the appropriate work because they had been appointed as leaders; they were recognized as leaders because they were seen to be doing the work." The organization was extremely simple and bore no resemblance to the system of hierarchical rule that subsequently developed.

Whether or not tension and misunderstanding had arisen in the church, the apostle gently urged the believers to "know" or to recognize with appreciation those who had been divinely selected as leaders of the community. C. F. Hogg and W. E. Vine, in *The Epistles of Paul the Apostle to the Thessalonians*, emphasized that such a recognition is "a purely spiritual exercise possible only to spiritual persons. Non-spiritual persons cannot recognize, and would not acknowledge, spiritual workers or their work" (177). Perhaps this is one reason for tensions in many local churches today. It is noteworthy that Paul referred to a plurality of elders and not to one leader alone. The centralization in one person of all the responsibilities of the church is not a New Testament concept.

The apostle described the work of the elders as laboring among the Christians, as presiding over them, and as admonishing them, the three present-tense participles being governed by a single definite article, thus making it clear that the three activities were those of one group of men. There is no indication that these leaders were set apart completely for the work; presumably they continued in their normal secular employment and did not depend on the church for their financial support (although 1 Timothy 5:17 implies that in particular circumstances such support was forthcoming in some churches).

The elders labored among their fellow-believers. This may, of course, have involved any form of service, although the primary reference must obviously have been to their spiritual work: teaching, shepherding, and caring generally for the spiritual needs of the members of the church. In 1 Timothy 5:17 the apostle specifically stressed "labour in the word and doctrine." The word *labour* might more accurately be rendered "toil" (as in 1:3) and implies strenuous effort in the light of potential difficulties and even opposition. Elsewhere the apostle used the same term of his own work (1 Corinthians 15:10; Galatians 4:11; Philippians 2:16; Colossians 1:29). The leaders were to be men who were prepared to sacrifice ease and comfort in order to care for the spiritual needs of the church. They were to be willing to engage in any service, however menial, that might further the spiritual life and welfare of God's people.

Second, the elders presided over the church "in the Lord." While their spiritual labors demanded honor and respect, it was also essential that their rule should be acknowledged. They were not, as one writer points out, secular leaders dealing with civic or political affairs; their work and leadership were spiritual. As in the Jewish setting, eldership connoted rule and presidency. No church will flourish without godly leaders to inspire and to guide. Also, as in the Jewish community, eldership implied the responsibility to exercise discipline where necessary; that was possible only if the elders were acknowledged to have spiritual authority.

When leadership was "in the Lord," personal ambition had no place. Spiritual maturity and the grace of Christ were vital in the exercise of such rule. Both leaders and those led were bound together in Christian bonds and in the love of Christ. Without that their rule would be ineffective.

Third, the elders functioned in the admonition of God's people. Although this involved discipline, it applied primarily to the reminding of individuals of something they were in danger of forgetting and which might result in failure or deficiency. In the warmth of Christian love, the elder appealed to the conscience and sought to save believers from wrongdoing or from an improper attitude in some matter.

For their work of this character, the elders were to be esteemed very highly in love. Because of what they did on behalf of the church, the warm and affectionate esteem of their fellow-believers should naturally be their reward. When harmonious relations of this nature existed it was not surprising that much blessing resulted.

Interrelationships

Be at peace among yourselves. But we exhort you, brethren, admonish the disorderly, encourage the fainthearted, support the weak, be patient toward all. See that no one renders unto anyone evil in return for evil, but always follow after what is good, one toward another, and toward all (5:13b-15).

The apostle Paul frequently enjoined peace on the churches he had planted or in which he had some personal interest (Romans 12:18; 14:19; 2 Corinthians 13:11; Ephesians 4:3; Colossians 3:15; 2 Timothy 2:22), and he here enjoined the Thessalonian believers to be at peace among themselves. There was no suggestion that this was not already their practice; the present imperative tended to imply that the apostle's desire was that they should continue to maintain what was already in existence. The counsel he had just given about the attitude to elders may have added emphasis to his exhortation. But if the church was to be blessed, a quiet peaceful relationship among the members was essential.

There followed a series of exhortations about different types of Christians. First of all, the "disorderly" were to be admonished. Moffatt rendered the word "loafers" and Barclay "lazy." The term was originally used of a soldier who deserted the ranks; it might justifiably be translated as "quitter." As has been noted, in Thessalonica some evidently had become so obsessed with the hope of the Lord's coming that they could think of nothing else. They had given up their employment and were without any means of subsistence. They had given way to habits of idleness and carelessness and had developed into busybodies, meddling with the affairs of others, and looking to the church for eleemosynary help instead of attempting to support themselves. G. Milligan in *St. Paul's Epistles to the Thessalonians* said that they were church members "who, without any intention of actual wrongdoing, were neglecting their daily duties, and falling into idle and careless habits, because of their expectation of the immediate *parousia* of the Lord" (154). Such individuals brought discredit on the church and on the Lord. The Christian was not to be slothful in business and was responsible to provide for the needs of himself and his family. Justifiably, those persons were to be admonished and instructed to resume a more orderly and honorable mode of life.

There were also others in the church whose need was different. Possibly discouraged by circumstances or fearful because of the threat of persecution, timidity might be overcome and they might stand confidently for the truth. (The AV rendering, "comfort the feeble minded," in seventeenth-century English refers to those whom we might describe as "fainthearted.")

The church also contained some who were "weak," not physically, of course, but morally or spiritually. W. Neil said that the presence of weak believers was "no Thessalonian peculiarity. . . . Weak souls are the normally frail human stuff of which the Christian church consists" (124-25). Hogg and Vine remarked, "Some believers are weak through lack of knowledge of the will of God, some through lack of courage to trust God, some, who are timorous or over-scrupulous, hesitate to use their liberty in Christ, some, through lack of stability or purpose, are easily carried away, some lack courage to face, or will to endure, persecution or criticism, some are unable to control the appetites of the body or the impulses of the mind" (183). Some, indeed, may have been those referred to in 1 Thessalonians 4:3-7, who were faced with the temptation to lapse into immorality. In whatever category they fell, these Christians obviously needed help, and the apostle urged the church to encourage and strengthen them.

Moreover, the apostle enjoined patience or longsuffering with all. This was one of the major qualities of Christian grace, included in Galatians 5:22 as among the fruits of the Spirit. There was no place here for anger or irritation or the desire for retaliation. Whatever the circumstances, believers were to demonstrate that spirit. It was to be evidenced, said one writer, "whether weak or strong, whether they try you by their presumption or timidity, by rude aggressiveness or by feebleness and incapacity."

Patience was to be shown to all. The spirit of longsuffering was exemplified in Christ and should be seen in His people (1 Timothy 1:16).

Then, surprisingly, Paul directed the Thessalonians to "see that no one
renders unto anyone evil in return for evil." The temptation to retaliate
was a characteristic of the natural man, but such an attitude was not for
Christians. They were to be constantly on their guard against any possibility of attempting to pay back a person who had done them an injury. The
law of Moses had provided for reimbursement of a wrong or injury—an
eye for an eye, and a tooth for a tooth—but our Lord introduced a new
standard in the sermon on the mount (Matthew 5:38-48). Here the apostle
categorically prohibited the spirit of resentment and retaliation, in words
addressed to the entire church.

By contrast, they were constantly to pursue what was good toward one
another and toward all. The reference was not to the pursuit of morality
for themselves. The apostle's intention was that they should seek the
good of others and attempt to do whatever was beneficial to them. The
mosaic law had said, "You shall love your neighbor," but the master
enunciated a new principle: "Love your enemies, bless those who curse
you, do good to those who hate you, and pray for those who despitefully
use you and persecute you" (Matthew 5:43-44). It was such behavior that
Paul was counseling. In their attitude to each other and to the unconverted around them, the Thessalonian Christians were to seek the welfare
of all with whom they came into contact. The selflessness of the master
Himself was to be reflected in the lives and conduct of His own people. It
was a high standard, but the only possible one for a Christian.

Communion

*Rejoice always. Pray without ceasing. Give thanks in everything: for
this is God's will in Christ Jesus for you (5:16-18).*

The Thessalonians were already enduring persecution, and it was evident
that greater trials lay ahead. They might well have been downcast and
despondent at the realization of the price to be paid for their adherence to
the faith. But the apostle exhorted them always to rejoice. It has often
been pointed out that this is the keynote of his epistle to the Philippians
(Philippians 4:4), written from prison and during personal experience of
tribulation and persecution. He had proved that suffering was not incom-

patible with rejoicing and, in fact, had discovered a wellspring of joy in Christ's love. Christian joy is not dependent on circumstances and is not affected by trial and difficulty. It springs from the unfathomable depths of divine blessing. This is no natural virtue; it derives from no human amiability. It is the product of the presence and power in life of the Holy Spirit. The Christian's heart rises above circumstances to rejoice in God, the source and inspiration of all true joy.

The believers were also exhorted to pray without ceasing. To do so did not imply a constant engaging in the act of prayer, but rather the cultivation of constant communion with God, the maintenance of a reverential approach to Him. The concept was not restricted to an outpouring of petitions for gifts or blessings, but rather it covered a whole range of communion—praise, thanksgiving, worship, adoration, as well as specific requests for help and blessing. Christians are children of God and it is natural that we should desire at all times to be in the presence of our Father and to be able to share all the circumstances of life with Him. He is not restricted to time or place; communion with the Father is possible in all circumstances and at all times (Colossians 1:3).

Further, the apostle exhorted, "Give thanks in everything." With a limited appreciation of life's ways and conditions, Christians might well be discouraged or depressed. But if the words of Romans 8:28 are true, then the injunction to give thanks in every circumstance becomes the obvious course. We are not called on to give thanks *for* everything, but *in* everything. In the awareness of our Lord's presence with us, with the consciousness of the power of the indwelling Spirit and with the appreciation of the boundless wealth of the Father's love, believers can give thanks in every circumstance and condition. It has been said that prayer and thanksgiving are the two wings of the soul, by which it soars upward to heaven.

The justification for the triplet of commands thus given was clearly stated, "This is God's will in Christ Jesus for you." It has been argued by a number of expositors that these words relate only to the last injunction, particularly as the pronoun *this* is singular. But, as D. E. Hiebert remarked, "The three commands are sufficiently homogeneous in character to allow their inclusion under the singular" (242). Collectively, they constitute the form of true devotion, and could scarcely be separated from each other. It is God's will that this character should be formed in His people.

Spiritual Life

Do not quench the Spirit. Do not despise prophesyings (5:19-20).

Scripture frequently refers to the Holy Spirit and His activities under the symbol of fire (e.g. Isaiah 4:4). John the Baptist declared that our Lord would baptize with the fire of the Holy Spirit (Matthew 3:11). When the divine paraclete descended at Pentecost, His presence was indicated by "cloven tongues like as of fire" (Acts 2:3). Literal fire may be extinguished or quenched so as to become inactive. Similarly, the apostle indicated that the operation of the Holy Spirit in the individual or in the community could be arrested or obstructed by the actions or attitude of those concerned. In all His power and energy, He indwells the believer, but it is only too possible for His work to be hindered by the one over whom He should have complete control. Therefore, the apostle Paul admonished the Thessalonians not to quench the Holy Spirit. It has been argued that his imperative related to the injunction immediately following and that some members of the church were stifling the Spirit's activities by their refusal to accept prophesyings. This interpretation is sustainable grammatically, but the apostle's words could well have been intended in a wider and more general sense. It is possible for believers in many ways to frustrate the divine purpose and to refuse to allow the Holy Spirit His way in their lives.

These words were followed by an exhortation not to despise prophesyings. It is improbable that Paul was alluding to the exercise of predictive powers. The concept of the prophet was not restricted to one who was divinely inspired to foretell the future. In the New Testament particularly, the etymological significance is of *forthtelling* rather than *foretelling*. The New Testament prophet (as also the Old Testament prophet in many instances) revealed what was otherwise hidden in the mind of God. He thus became the mouthpiece of God for a particular purpose or revelation. The apostle later encouraged the Corinthian believers to desire spiritual gifts, but placed that of prophecy in preference to all others (1 Corinthians 14:1). It was logical that he should tell the Thessalonians not to despise or think lightly of this gift.

It has been argued by some writers that the church at Thessalonica had erred in trying to guard against the disorders which occurred later in the church at Corinth through the uncontrolled use of the charismatic gifts. That suggestion seems somewhat doubtful. A more natural meaning of the apostle's words was that the revelation of God's mind and purpose through spiritual ministry was not to be ignored.

J. Robertson's comments in *The Early Religion of Israel* are worth quoting. He said, "The prophets had a practical office to discharge. It was part of their commission to show the people of God 'their transgressions, and the house of Jacob their sins' (Isaiah 58:1; Ezekiel 22:2; 43:10; Micah 3:8). They were, therefore, pastors and ministerial monitors of the people of God. It was their duty to admonish and reprove, to denounce prevailing sins, to threaten the people with the terrors of divine judgment, and to call them to repentance. They also brought the message of consolation and pardon (Isaiah 40:1,2). They were the watchmen set upon the walls of Zion to blow the trumpet, and give timely warning of approaching danger (Ezekiel 3:17; 33:7-9; Jeremiah 6:17; Isaiah 62:6)" (461).

It is a mistake to contend that the Old Testament prophet's functions have no counterpart in the New Testament. In many respects the functions bear a marked similarity. If the New Testament prophet is spiritually gifted by the Holy Spirit, was it not true that the Old Testament prophet was guided and "borne along" by the same Spirit?

The New Testament prophets, as another writer said, "were the human channels through whom the Spirit made known His will and purpose for His people. The prophetic revelation might at times concern the future (Acts 11:28), but not necessarily so. The prophetic message generally was in the nature of instruction and guidance concerning the present (Acts 13:2)." The Thessalonian Christians were to pay full heed to God's message through their prophets and not to disparage it.

Reality

> But test all things; hold fast what is good. Abstain from every kind of evil (5:21-22).

Without giving any specific criteria here, Paul counseled his readers to prove or test everything—not merely the words of the prophets to which he had just alluded. It was a principle for the whole of their Christian lives. They were not to accept anything blindly, but to exercise the spiritual judgment bestowed on them.

Having done so, the natural consequence ensued. They should hold fast what was good and, by inference, reject everything else. Their spiritual discernment would guide them to accept what was intrinsically genuine, whether in regard to ministry and prophesying, or to general conduct of life.

Further, again naturally following the previous clause, they were to abstain from every kind of evil. The AV rendering of "every appearance of evil" has led to the conclusion that the injunction was to refrain from anything that looked like evil, but this was not the apostle's meaning. Findlay suggested that the meaning was rather to "abstain from every evil sight or show, i.e., from all that is evil in the outward show of things about you." J. N. Darby translated, "Hold aloof from every form of wickedness." Christians are sanctified to God and their lives should be pure and holy.

Sanctification

Now may the God of peace Himself sanctify you completely; and may your spirit and soul and body be preserved in entirety without blame unto the coming of our Lord Jesus Christ. Faithful is He who calls you, who will also do it (5:23-24).

In spite of all the personal efforts of his readers, the apostle realized that their maintenance of a life in conformity with God's will could never be effective without divine help. Consequently he prayed that the God of peace would Himself sanctify them completely (or to full perfection). They were, of course, already sanctified by the blood of Calvary, but he was here concerned not with their standing before God, but with their daily condition. His prayer was for their *practical* sanctification. He desired that they might be pure and holy in every respect and at every level, fully aware that this could be achieved only by the cleansing power of God.

In greater detail, the petition continued that their spirit and soul and body might be preserved in entirety and blamelessly unto (or in) the coming of our Lord Jesus Christ. The term *entirety* or *full integrity* was used in the Septuagint version of Deuteronomy 27:6 concerning the stones to be used in building the altar (AV "whole stones"). The apostle yearned for their complete sanctification during the entire course of their lives until they were removed to glory at the coming of Christ for His church.

It has been maintained strenuously by some commentators that verse 23 gives no support for the view that man is a trichotomy, but it is difficult to interpret it in any other way. Findlay said, "It is not necessary to regard 'spirit and soul and body' as three distinct logical divisions of man's nature." Yet he commented that "the *spirit* is kept, when no evil reaches the inner depths of man's nature, or disturbs his relations to God and eternity; his *soul*, when the world of self is guarded, when all his feelings and thoughts are sinless; his *body*, when his outward life and relations to the material world are innocent."

The Bible regards the soul as the seat of affections, desires, lusts, and motives, and as the basis for the will (e.g., 1 Samuel 18:1; Psalm 84:2; Job 30:25). The soul is the real ego and is closely identified with the person. The soul and spirit are closely connected but are distinguishable from each other (Hebrews 4:12). The spirit is evidently our higher consciousness. If the soul is the medium of self-consciousness, the spirit is the means of God-consciousness and of communication with Him. The body is the physical frame by which others are aware of the person and is therefore the medium of contact with the world. At death, both soul and spirit leave the body (Genesis 35:18; Matthew 27:50). Paul's desire was that the whole being might be preserved without blame or blemish until the coming of Christ.

God had called the Thessalonians to lives of dedication to Himself. Paul declared that not only would God call, but He would also effectively accomplish His purpose (cf. Numbers 23:19). His object was to transform His people into the likeness of Christ until their perfect glorification with Him (2 Corinthians 3:18; Colossians 3:4).

Conclusion

Brethren, pray also for us. Salute all the brethren with a holy kiss. I adjure you by the Lord that this epistle be read to all the brethren. The grace of our Lord Jesus Christ be with you (5:25-28).

The apostle and his colleagues prayed for their converts. Now, they themselves sought the prayer support of the Thessalonian Christians. In spite of his ability and gifts, Paul was conscious of his dependence on God and of his need of the prayer fellowship of others. He repeatedly sought their prayers (Ephesians 6:19; Colossians 4:3-4; Philippians 1:19; Romans 15:30). The difficulties that the missionary band was experiencing and the active opposition with which they were so often confronted fully justified his plea for prayer on their behalf.

"Salute all the brethren with a holy kiss." This form of greeting was universal in the early church and is still preserved in eastern churches. It has almost died out in the west, although it is still practiced in some European countries. The apostle made it clear that the gesture was a sacred one; it was to be a *holy* kiss, which would attract no criticism or suspicion. It was commonly bestowed after the communion service or breaking of bread; hence the Greek church has included it as part of the service.

There followed a solemn adjuration that the epistle should be read to all the brethren, presumably to all the church. It was to be read aloud publicly. The reason for this request, unique in Paul's epistles, is not obvious. A. von Harnack suggested that the letter was received by the gentile believers at Thessalonica and that, without this request, the Jewish converts might not have had the benefit of its teaching, but his is a doubtful argument. Others have concluded that parties had arisen in the church and that some might have been excluded from hearing the letter, but there is no indication in either epistle of sectarianism such as later arose at Corinth. The apostle may have desired to ensure that those whom he had admonished, like the idlers and loafers, would be aware of what had been said. But speculation gives no satisfactory explanation. The adjuration was "by the Lord" and was, therefore, a serious matter. In any case, the character of the epistle was such that every member of the church stood in need of the teaching; it was imperative that they should not be denied it.

The epistle concluded with a very brief benediction, "The grace of our Lord Jesus Christ be with you." This was expanded in other letters but it did, in fact, convey all that was necessary. It superseded the formal "Farewell" of the normal heathen conclusion to a letter and contained virtually all the blessing from which believers could benefit. The AV addition of *amen* was seemingly supplied by a copyist and is not regarded as authentic.

10

A Second Letter

2 Thessalonians 1:1-12

It is rather surprising to find that after a lapse of probably only two or three months Paul and his colleagues addressed a second letter to the church at Thessalonica. The Pauline authorship was unhesitatingly accepted by the early church; it was not until the beginning of the nineteenth century that any question was raised. It was then argued that an alleged difference in the eschatological teaching of the two epistles obviously indicated different authorship. The argument was flimsy, but considerable discussion ensued because of the authority of those who presented it. But, as K. C. Lake stated in *Contemporary Thinking About Paul*, research has since served "decisively to remove the eschatological argument from the list of possible objections to the authenticity of 2 Thessalonians" (235).

As already mentioned, A. von Harnack proposed that the first epistle was sent to the gentile community in the church, and the second epistle to the Jewish section of the church. Not only has this suggestion no substance, but it would be totally unlike the apostle Paul—who so strongly condemned disunity in the church at Corinth—to foster separate parties at Thessalonica.

In his *Studies in the Gospels and Epistles*, T. W. Manson argued that the second epistle was written before the first (267) but the reasons put forward have found little support. It is practically universally agreed today that the canonical order is correct.

The consensus of scholarship accepts the Pauline authorship of the epistle, its complete authenticity, and its chronological place as second to 1 Thessalonians. It seems clear, moreover, that it was written shortly after the first epistle, probably in A.D. 51, and was composed in Corinth.

It seems probable that further information had reached the apostle about the condition of the Thessalonian church: the problems under discussion there, and the persecution confronting the believers. Whether the news had been conveyed by members of the church or by other believers is not known. The commercial connections between Thessalonica and Corinth would, in any case, have facilitated communication. It is clear that in some way news had reached Paul of the erroneous interpretation that was being given to the day of the Lord and its timing, and also about the continued reprehensible conduct of some members of the church. It was essential that a more careful eschatological explanation be given and also that a more serious admonition be conveyed to those who had seemingly paid no heed to the injunctions given in the first letter. These were the primary reasons for the second letter.

Paul, Silas, and Timothy were not again associated in the New Testament record after Paul's departure from Corinth. The fact that they were united in the salutation is a confirmation that, like the first epistle, the second was written from Corinth. The difference in style is doubtless due at least partly to the fact that in the first letter the apostle was compelled to defend himself against attempts to assassinate his character. That did not apply when he was writing the second letter, which probably accounts for its less emotional character.

Salutation

Paul and Silvanus and Timotheus to the church of the Thessalonians in God our Father and the Lord Jesus Christ. Grace to you and peace from God the Father and the Lord Jesus Christ (1:1-2).

Apart from the addition of the word *our* before the first *Father*, the salutation in the second letter is identical with that in the first. As already indicated, some versions omit the last nine words in 1 Thessalonians 1:1, but it seems more than probable that they were included as in the second letter, bringing the salutation into line with other Pauline letters.

Thanksgiving

We are bound to give thanks to God for you always, brethren, as it is meet, because your faith grows exceedingly, and the love of each one of you all toward one another abounds; so that we ourselves boast of you in the churches of God for your patience and faith in all your persecutions and the afflictions which you are enduring (1:3-4).

The apostle's thanksgiving in his second epistle was more comprehensive than in the first. In fact, at first reading, the commendation seems almost excessive. The Thessalonians' spiritual growth and development, and the steadfastness they had displayed in severe persecution and tribulation, involved a deep sense of gratitude to God in the missionaries' hearts. Not only was it fitting and due to them, but the apostle felt compelled to give thanks to God for them. Their missionary work had not been in vain; these converts were exemplifying much that they had been taught.

The report brought earlier by Timothy had encouraged the apostle's heart, but later news had reached him regarding the spiritual growth of the Thessalonian converts. The growth of their faith seemed to him to be beyond all natural expectation—and, by implication, to be due solely to the work of God in them. Not only was their faith growing exceedingly but their love toward each other abounded, as he had prayed that it might (1 Thessalonians 3:12). J. B. Lightfoot, in *Notes on the Epistles of St. Paul*, suggested that the verbs used implied an inner organic growth of their faith, but an outward diffusion of their love like a flood irrigating the land (98). Each one of them demonstrated unreserved affection to all of the others. It was a super-abounding love.

Paul and his colleagues did not boast of themselves or of their work, but the news of the spiritual state of the church at Thessalonica gave them cause for boasting of others. The emphasis in the use of the two pronouns *we ourselves* is somewhat unusual, but was possibly an incidental stressing of the apostle's exuberance in glorying in others. The missionary band obviously reported far and wide what had happened in Thessalonica to other churches.

There was justification for their boasting. Trials had befallen these young Christians such as they had probably never anticipated. Active hostility from the enemies of the gospel proved fierce and bitter. Yet they consistently and resolutely maintained their trust in God. Their endurance and faith were sorely tested, but bore up under the severest strain. As one writer commented, they bravely held "themselves erect and firm under the sufferings endured because of their faith." The patience referred to does not denote meek submissiveness but rather heroic endurance closely linked to their faith.

In the light of all that was happening in the Thessalonian church, there was justification for the apostolic thanksgiving.

Retribution

This is a manifest token of the righteous judgment of God, to the end that you may be counted worthy of the kingdom of God, for which you also are suffering; since it is a righteous thing with God to recompense affliction to those who afflict you and, to you who are afflicted, rest with us, at the revelation of the Lord Jesus from heaven with His mighty angels, in flaming fire, rendering vengeance to those who do not know God and who do not obey the gospel of our Lord Jesus. They will pay the penalty of eternal destruction from the presence of the Lord and from the glory of His power, when He comes to be glorified in His saints and to be marveled at in all those who believed (because our testimony to you was believed) on that day (1:5-10).

The steadfastness of the Thessalonians under the stress of persecution was a plain indication that new life and power had been imparted to them. Seeking to do the will of God had brought them suffering for their faith, but by the courage and fortitude their heavenly Father had inspired in them, they had demonstrated true Christian character. This was therefore a manifest token of the ultimate divine judgment. As Findlay remarked, "The rapture of the Christian martyrs at the stake was a sign of God's presence with them and an omen of retribution to their enemies." Their suffering evidenced plainly that they were accounted worthy of the kingdom of God. Their sufferings were being endured for the sake of the kingdom (cf. 2 Timothy 2:12). The glory to come was full compensation for the present loss.

But there was to be a recompense: the future day of judgment at Christ's return. The remainder of this brief section is the first piece of eschatological teaching in this second epistle. It has frequently been pointed out that there is evidence that the early church collated the Old Testament references to the coming of the Lord. As T. F. Glasson said in *The Second Advent*, "The Christians took over the O. T. doctrine of the Advent of the Lord, making the simple adjustment that the Lord was the Lord Jesus" (176). Paul was well aware of the contents of this collection, which developed into a growing tradition, and undoubtedly drew from the collection for use in this section of the epistle.

Retribution was just, and in accordance with divine principles. God's dealings with human beings are not capricious nor are His actions arbitrary. The course He takes is always just and equitable. Accordingly, the apostle affirmed that it was "a righteous thing with God to recompense affliction to those who" afflicted His people (cf. Isaiah 66:6). God would mete out strict justice; evil conduct would be fully requited. Those who attacked God's people would suffer for their malevolence and antagonism. On the other hand, those who had suffered would be granted relief from the tension and strain of their tribulations.

These actions were in complete conformity with moral justice and would occur at the revelation of the Lord Jesus from heaven. The reference was not to our Lord's coming to the air to translate His church from earth to heaven (1 Thessalonians 4:16-17), but to His return to earth in power and glory (Revelation 19:11-21). As William Kelly wrote in *The Epistles of Paul the Apostle to the Thessalonians*, "It is not the action of sovereign grace which translates the saints waiting for Him to heaven, but the display of judicial righteousness by the Lord when He appears in glory" (89).

When that occurs, the Lord will be accompanied by His mighty angels (or "the angels of His power") and in flaming fire (cf. Exodus 3:2; Acts 7:30). He will be seen in all His majesty and splendor as He returns to execute justice and to render vengeance (i.e., complete justice, not vindictiveness) "to those who do not know God and who do not obey the gospel of our Lord Jesus Christ." Although the apostle referred primarily to the persecutors of God's people at Thessalonica, the judgment he envisaged will, of course, have universal application.

The culpability of those who do not know God and do not obey the gospel naturally varies in degree and in accordance with their measure of light and opportunity. Those who are fully aware of the claims of Christ obviously have far greater responsibility than those whose lot has been cast in darkest paganism. But both are reprehensible for ignoring the light they have, and they must pay the penalty.

The final judgment was described as "the penalty of eternal destruction from the presence of the Lord and from the glory of His power." The penalty is, as W. Neil remarked, a "punishment determined by a lawful process." The sentence implies permanent banishment from the divine presence and glory (Revelation 20:15). Eternal destruction is the antithesis of eternal life (John 5:24,29), but it does not imply the cessation of existence. Findlay remarked, "There is no sufficient reason for interpreting the destruction of the reprobate as signifying their annihilation, or extinction of being; they will be lost for ever—lost to God and goodness. Nor can we limit the range of the word *eternal* in its relation to this fearful doom; it removes all limit of time, and is the express opposite of *temporary* (2 Corinthians 4:18). Seventy-two times the Greek original of the adjective is found in the N. T.; forty-four of these examples are repetitions of the phrase 'eternal life'; it is arbitrary to suppose that, in the opposite combination, 'eternal' bears a restricted sense. Christ's judicial words in Matthew 25:46 bar all attempts to minimize the penal effect of the sentence of the Last Day: 'eternal punishment,' He says, and 'eternal life.' Compare Philippians 3:19, 'whose *end* is destruction.'"

The word *aionios* literally means age-long and denotes an endless, undefined period. H. B. Swete said that 2 Thessalonians 1:9 is "the most express statement in Paul's epistles of the eternity of future punishment." Some commentators have endeavored to restrict the meaning of *aionios* to a qualitative aspect, but C. J. Ellicott in *A Critical and Grammatical Commentary on St. Paul's Epistles to the Thessalonians* maintained that "the early Greek expositors never appear to have lost sight of its quantitative aspect." The eternally lost are banished for ever "from the presence [or face] of the Lord and from the glory of His power." If the causal force of *apo* (from) is assumed, the significance is that their doom is meted out to them from that glorious majesty. But the generally accepted view is that the reference is to their exclusion from heaven and to their permanent separation from that glory. They will be irrevocably separated from God. E. J. Bicknell said in *The First and Second Epistles to the Thessalonians* that this "sums the Christian doctrine of hell. Heaven is primarily the presence of God. Hell is the loss of that presence (cf. Luke 13:27)" (70).

Our Lord's coming will have a dual purpose, however. He will come not only as judge to recompense evildoers for their crimes, but also to be glorified in His saints. In His prayer uttered in the garden, our Lord said of His disciples, "I am glorified in them" (John 17:10). In the day of His manifestation, His glory will be reflected in the myriads of His people who accompany Him to earth. Completely transformed into His image, those hosts will show the transcendent splendor of their Lord. The whole angelic hierarchy will then look on that scene in wonder. Even now they seek to understand the meaning of His dealings with earth, but as they gaze on that incomparable presentation of their sovereign's glory in the multitudes of redeemed human beings, they will marvel at the divine purposes and at what has been achieved. The spectators may also include the unbelieving world, but Paul went no further in any identification.

The revelation will be in all who have believed. Parenthetically, the apostle reminded the Thessalonians that they would be among the company because they had believed the missionaries' message to them.

All this was to occur in the day of our Lord's appearing. The one who was once despised and rejected, who was accorded a cross of shame, is yet to return to the world as king of kings and lord of lords. God's vindication of His Son will then be plain to all.

Prayer Fellowship

To which end also we constantly pray for you, that our God may count you worthy of His calling and fulfill every desire of goodness and work of faith in power, that the name of our Lord Jesus may be glorified in you, and you in Him, according to the grace of our God and the Lord Jesus Christ (1:11-12).

The glorious prospect, which he had held out before his readers, motivated the apostle to pray for them constantly. Because ethical implications attended the hope of the future, Paul was concerned that the converts might live in the light of their high calling. He yearned that the holiness and practical sanctification befitting the people of God might be manifest in them, so that God could justifiably regard them as worthy of His calling. Paul frequently referred to the divine call in his writings; the tacit implication of his words to the Thessalonians was parallel to his exhortation to the Ephesians to walk worthily of the calling wherewith they were called (Ephesians 4:1).

Paul's second petition indicated the means that God would adopt in producing the character for which the apostle prayed. Only He could bring to fulfillment all their diverse desires for goodness. Only He could develop their work of faith, the outward complement of their inward desires.

The ultimate purpose of the apostle's prayer was that the name of the Lord Jesus might be glorified in them, that Christ, in all His glory and fullness, might be seen unveiled in these believers, that His character might be manifested in their lives and conduct.

But the process was to be reciprocal: they were to be glorified in Christ, if the prayer was to be answered. Hiebert said, "This mutual glorification implies the essential unity between the Lord and His own, brought to its consummation at the Second Advent. The manifestation of the saints in glory awaits Christ's return in glory (Colossians 3:4)" (297). Or, as W. F. Adeney put it, "The servants come in for a share of the honour of the master whose livery they wear."

That wonderful result for those who were then suffering persecution and tribulation was to be "according to the grace of our God and the Lord Jesus Christ." The believer was called in grace and is maintained in grace. His spiritual progression comes from the grace of God operating in his life; his ultimate "translation" to glory is the result of grace. The answer to the apostle's prayer was in accordance with divine grace.

11

The Mystery of Iniquity

2 Thessalonians 2:1-12

T he primary reason for the second
epistle is made clear in 2:1-12,
the substance of which was of
great eschatological significance. Although directed to correcting a misunderstanding or misinterpretation, it obviously supplemented oral
teaching given by the missionaries when at Thessalonica. For us, without
a knowledge of what had been taught orally, interpretation is naturally
somewhat more difficult. The section contains a revelation of certain
events of the future, details of which are not found elsewhere in the
Pauline writings. At the same time there are reflections of Old Testament
phraseology and teaching.

The bitter persecutions through which the Thessalonian believers were
passing had led some of them to the conclusion that they were already
experiencing the tribulation and judgment of the day of the Lord. Because
of the effect on their stability and spiritual attitude, it was essential that
such an impression should be corrected, and that the apostle proceeded
to do.

Erroneous Views

*Now we beseech you, brethren, by the coming of our Lord Jesus
Christ and our gathering together unto Him, to the end that you be*

not quickly shaken from your mind, nor yet be kept in alarm, either
by spirit or by word, or by epistle as from us, as that the day of the
Lord is now present (2:1-2).

The mistaken apprehension that the day of the Lord, which Paul had
stated would arrive unexpectedly, catching many unawares, had already
arrived had thrown the Thessalonians into a state of bewilderment and
anxiety. In his first epistle, Paul had explained that that dreadful period of
judgment would *not* overtake the Christians like a thief and that God had
not appointed them to wrath (1 Thessalonians 5:4-9). That should have
sufficed to avoid any precipitate or ill-considered ideas, such as those
that now affected them. But the sufferings through which they were passing were so intense that it seemed as if nothing could possibly exceed
them. Their experience convinced the Thessalonians that the unprece-
dented period of trial had actually come upon them. How otherwise
could their tribulations be explained?

Their mental agitation had resulted from a too hasty conclusion about
the meaning of events, yet there was some justification for it. Apparently
there had been a prophetic utterance on the subject in the church, al-
legedly inspired by the Holy Spirit (or perhaps by some other spirit).
Some people, on the other hand, were influenced by the spoken word of
one or more of the teachers in the church, who possibly had attempted to
explain Old Testament prophecy in relation to current conditions. In
addition, it seems that a spurious letter had reached the church, purport-
ing to have been sent by the apostle Paul, which confirmed the misap-
prehensions that had arisen.

Paul therefore asked his readers not to allow their equilibrium to be
disturbed by spirit, word, or false epistle (or even by a misinterpretation
of his first epistle). At the moment, as Neil said, "they were behaving like
ships that had been insecurely anchored, had broken from their moorings, and were now blown hither and thither with every rumor or chance
remark" (157). It was a state of undesirable instability.

The apostle based his appeal on "the coming of our Lord Jesus Christ
and our gathering together unto Him," i.e., on the events he had so clearly
described in 1 Thessalonians 4:15-17. Those eagerly anticipated events
related to the church, whereas (as he had lucidly explained in 1 Thessalonians 5) the day of the Lord did not. The latter applied to the children of
darkness and not to the Christians, children of the light. Now Paul directed their attention to the Christian hope and away from the judgments
of a subsequent period.

A number of expositors have tried to relate the events of the succeeding verses to the subject matter of 2:1, arguing that the coming of our Lord and the "translation" of the church cannot occur until after the manifestation of the "man of sin." The preposition *huper*, which the AV and some other versions render "by," has the significance of "in the interest of" or "on behalf of," and can justifiably be translated simply as "by." It is more difficult to justify the interpretation "with reference to" or "with regard to" or "as touching," all of which would give some support to the theory referred to above. It is more logical, and more correct, to regard 2:1 as referring to the events of the Christian's hope, in contrast to those mentioned in subsequent verses of chapter 2.

The aim of the appeal was that the Thessalonian Christians should not be so disturbed by the erroneous teaching being promulgated. They should be neither shaken (loosed from their moorings) nor troubled (shattered by the shock) by the mistaken conclusion that the dread day of the Lord was already present.

The current teaching in some quarters, that the rapture of the church cannot be expected until at least the end of the great tribulation, leads only to confusion similar to that at Thessalonica nineteen centuries ago.

The Apostasy

Let no man beguile you in any wise. That day will not come, except the apostasy comes first, and the man of lawlessness be revealed, the son of perdition, he who opposes and exalts himself over all that is called God or that is worshiped, so that he takes his seat in the temple of God, setting himself forth as God (2:3-4).

The apostle, well aware of the prevalence of false teachers in his day, warned them not to allow anyone to beguile them in any of the variety of ways so often employed. He recognized the general gullibility even of Christians (as of others). Findlay said that the word *beguile* or *deceive* "implies a *thorough, commonly a wicked, deception* (cf. Romans 16:18). The kindred noun (*deceit*) appears in verse 10." There was evidently a serious and determined effort to undermine the apostle's teaching and to rob the believers of their hope. Without a strong warning against those who were promulgating this misleading concept, the delusion was liable to persist.

The words "that day will not come" do not appear in the original, but are properly supplied by the translators to complete the sense. An ellipsis of this kind is common in Greek, as evident in the Pauline writings also.

Before the period of the day of the Lord commenced, the apostle revealed, another event must occur, which he described as "the apostasy," or "the rebellion." F. F. Bruce said:

> It appears probable from the context that a general abandonment of the basis of civil order is envisaged . . . it is a large-scale revolt against public order, and since public order is maintained by the "governing authorities" who "have been instituted by God," any assault on it is an assault on a divine ordinance (Romans 13:1-2). It is, in fact, the whole concept of divine authority over the world that is set at defiance in "the rebellion" par excellence (167).

The term used, *he apostasia*, is the one from which the English word *apostasy* is derived. Hiebert said:

> It denotes a deliberate abandonment of a formerly professed position or view, a defection, a rejection of a former allegiance. In classical Greek it was used to denote a political or military rebellion; in the Septuagint it was used of rebellion against God (Joshua 22:22); in 1 Maccabees 2:15 it is used of the enforcement of apostasy to paganism. This religious connotation appears in the use of the term in the New Testament (Acts 21:21; 1 Timothy 4:1; 2 Timothy 3:1-9; 4:3-4; Hebrews 3:12). Obviously Paul's sign has reference to apostasy within the circle of the professed church (305).

It could, of course, apply equally well to apostasy in the religious world of any day.

Kenneth Wuest, J. R. Rice, E. Schuyler English, and others have propounded a view that has become popular: the word *apostasia* means simply a "departure" and that 2:3 refers not to a revolt against authority, but to the departure of the church at the Lord's coming. Attractive although the theory is, it is really not tenable. The church will not be translated (or depart from this planet) by its own initiative, but will be snatched away by the irresistible power of Christ. The apostle referred to a departure from the faith or a worldwide revolt against divine authority.

A further precursor to the day of judgment was described as "the man of lawlessness." Some commentators have seen this man as the culmination and personification of the apostasy, which is a reasonable interpretation. The appearance of this man will evidently be sudden; the verb *revealed* in 2:3 is in the aorist tense, indicating that the revelation will occur at a specific point in time and not be a gradual process. His emergence on the public stage will be in the character of the lawless one; prior to that he may have been completely unknown.

The apostle described him as "the son of perdition." Many have seized on this as an identification with Judas Iscariot, whom our Lord described in similar terms in John 17:12, but that association is obviously fallacious. Because of his character and conduct, and particularly by his betrayal of the master, Judas was irretrievably lost—the son of perdition. Similarly, the character and conduct of this mysterious personage of the future will place him in the same category—he is irrevocably doomed. But there is not the slightest reason for assuming the future revivification of Judas Iscariot to fill this role.

The great rebel of the future will engage in antitheistic and blasphemous activities. His deliberate policy will be to oppose all other religions, to exalt himself in opposition to every deity, true or false, who is worshiped. Doubtless the apostle had in mind (and had probably taught at Thessalonica) the attack on all forms of religion implied in Daniel 9:27, where the prophet disclosed that at a particular point in time (halfway through the period of the last seven years mentioned in that verse) all religious services and worship would suddenly be stopped by "the prince that shall come." Daniel indicated that this would introduce "the abomination of desolation," or the desolating idolatry. In His Olivet discourse, our Lord made it clear that "the abomination of desolation" was both an object (Matthew 24:15) and a person (Mark 13:14). The first reference presumably alludes to the statue of this man set up as an object of worship (Revelation 13:14-15). The second reference presumably alludes to the man personally and to his entry into the temple (described by Paul in 2 Thessalonians 2:4).

In A.D. 40 the Roman emperor Caligula attempted to set up his statue in the temple at Jerusalem as an assertion of his claim to divinity. The man of lawlessness is not only to have his statue erected at Jerusalem, but will himself enter the temple and demand to be acknowledged as divine. Since the penalty for refusal to pay homage to him will be death (Revelation 13:15), the majority of persons will doubtless render the desired submission.

The one of whom Paul wrote was no mere principle or abstraction. The apostle portrayed one before whom nations will one day bow and to whom rulers will submit. Attempts to identify him over the centuries have been numberless. Because he will oppose all deities and religious observances, some have illogically identified him with the pope or the papal system, but the fallacy of this is obvious. Neither the pope nor the papal system is opposed to religion. In recent years, it has sometimes been argued that Paul's reference was undoubtedly to communism, but communism is an ideology and the biblical picture is of a man.

Identification of the individual will plainly not be practicable until his appearance (after the rapture of the church). Certain means of identification are provided in Revelation 13, but these are for use at the appropriate time. There seems no probability of any recognition during the present church era. B. B. Warfield in his *Biblical and Theological Studies* insisted that the Pauline description "was fulfilled in the terrible story of the emperors of Rome" (472-73). But the man of lawlessness has not yet been revealed and is obviously an eschatological person.

Findlay maintained that "the apostasy" and "the man of lawlessness" must be distinguished, "in that the former is the corruption of *the church*, while the latter is the culmination of the evil of *the world*. . . . The former naturally contributes to the latter, an apostate church paving the way for the advent of an atheistic world power."

Having proscribed all religions and religious practices, the man of lawlessness, according to Paul, will take his seat in the temple of God, setting himself forth as God. It has been suggested by some expositors that the temple must refer to the Christian church (Ephesians 2:22) and that he will establish his authority in the church as a power base, but that suggestion runs counter to the destruction of the ecclesiastical system portrayed by John (Revelation 17:16), which will presumably occur at the time of the abolition of all religion and its replacement by the worship of this man. It seems plain that the reference was to the material temple at Jerusalem (cf. Matthew 24:15) and, since this was destroyed in A.D. 70, the implication is that a temple will be rebuilt there at some future date. The word *naos*, used by the apostle for the temple in 2:4, was employed of the innermost shrine, or "holy of holies" of the temple, where the shekinah glory rested between the cherubim of the ark. Evidently the audacious rebel will blasphemously take his seat in the *sanctum sanctorum* itself, the rightful shrine only of the eternal God.

The Restraint

Do you remember that, when I was yet with you, I used to tell you these things? And now you know that which restrains, to the end

that he may be revealed in his own season. For the mystery of
lawlessness is already in operation: only there is one who restrains
now until he is taken out of the way (2:5-7).

The apostle then made it clear that he was not discussing an entirely new
and perplexing subject. In an implicit mild reproof, he asked whether his
readers did not recall that he had explained these matters during the
period of the missionary band's stay in Thessalonica. If they had remembered that early teaching they would surely not have been thrown off
balance later by misleading teaching. (Since he had already taught them
the essence of the subject, there was no need now for any fuller or more
explicit statement.)

From the instruction they had received, they should have been aware
that the revelation of the man of lawlessness had not yet taken place and
that consequently the day of the Lord had not yet arrived. Indeed, the
apostle declared, they knew what was hindering his revelation. That information had been imparted to them in the course of the preaching at
Thessalonica.

Here Paul did not restate what had been taught, so the modern reader
is left with a problem of interpretation. It was clear that the almighty still
retained control of the situation and that there was a time in the divine
program for the emergence of this man to be permitted. There could be
no premature appearance of the final development of evil; a powerful
force held it in check and would continue to do so until the divinely
appointed time. Bounds were set, and nothing could pass those limits
until the hour struck.

Nevertheless, the mystery of lawlessness was already active. The spirit
that would later dominate the sinister individual was already operative in
creating the atmosphere and conditions for his coming. As Hiebert remarked, "It does not merely denote disorder and violation of law, but
rather that definite aim of the devil to overthrow the law of God and
establish his own rule" (312). The twentieth century jettisoning of moral
standards and conventions surely is an indication of the ceaseless activity
of evil forces to secure the desired end. But the full revelation has not yet
come.

The apostle further reminded the Thessalonian believers that there was
a second hindrance to the manifestation of the one who would later
plumb the depths of iniquity. There was "one who restrains now," as
distinct from the restraint in the previous verse. In 2:6 a neuter participle

is used with a neuter article in reference to the hindering or restraining; in 2:7 a masculine participle is used with a masculine article. The obvious implication is that the first restraint is a thing, whereas the second is a person. Moreover, the apostle stated incisively that the second restrainer will continue to prevent the appearance of the lawless one until he (the restrainer) is himself removed, or "taken out of the midst."

Attempts to identify the hindering influence to which Paul referred have been varied and ingenious. B. B. Warfield in *The Prophecies of St. Paul* concluded that the reference must be to the Jewish state, and that, until Christianity became completely distinct from Judaism, the bitterness of the imperial persecutions could not be experienced (473). It has been suggested that the restrainer is Satan, who will hold back the manifestation of his dupe until the appointed hour. Others have regarded the hindrance as the preaching of the gospel.

The tendency of most commentators is to interpret the words as referring to the Roman empire or to one or more of the Roman emperors. F. F. Bruce, for example, wrote:

> Paul viewed established government as imposing a salutary restraint on evil (Romans 13:3-4), and, in his mission field, established government meant effectively the Roman Empire, personally embodied in the emperor. . . . He knew that Roman rule would not last for ever, and that its benevolent neutrality could not be counted on indefinitely, but in the present situation a welcome curb was placed on the forces of lawlessness (171-72).

The interpretation is most commonly expressed as the control of law, initially in the empire and subsequently in general. Findlay said:

> The fabric of civil law and the authority of the magistrate formed a bulwark and breakwater against the excesses both of autocratic tyranny and of popular violence. For this power St. Paul had a profound respect (see Romans 13:1-7). . . . Nor did Roman law fall with the empire itself, any more than it rose from it. It has been in spirit, and to a large extent in substance, the parent of the legal systems of Christendom. . . . Let reverence for law disappear in public life, along with religious faith, and there is nothing to prevent a new Caesar becoming master and god of the civilized world, armed with infinitely greater power.

The argument that law restrains evil is somewhat open to question. The law decides when its enactments have been broken and imposes a sentence on the transgressor, but it does not prevent him from repeating his crime. Moreover, activities such as gambling, adultery, abortion, homosexuality, etc., although sins in the sight of God, may be legalized and thereupon cease to be crimes.

J. N. Darby in his *Notes on the Epistles to the Thessalonians* attempted to combine more than one view in his interpretation.

> The thing which restrained then is not that which restrains now. Then it was, in one sense, the Roman empire. . . . At present the hindrance is still the existence of the governments established by God in the world; and God will maintain them as long as there is here below the gathering of His church. Viewed in this light, the hindrance is, at the bottom, the presence of the church and of the Holy Spirit on the earth.

Although Darby's final conclusion may well be justified, it does not follow logically from his previous propositions.

As 2:9 indicates, the man of lawlessness will be inspired and dominated by Satan; he will receive diabolical power and authority (Revelation 13:2). The devil's centuries-long rebellion against God has been characterized consistently by the attempt to overthrow the ruler of divine law and order and to substitute unfettered lawlessness and to exercise his own rule. No human legislation or authority could restrict his activities or prevent the fulfillment of his ultimate aim. There is only one who has the power to restrain the operations of the devil and to keep sin and lawlessness under control. That, of course, is almighty God.

During this age (as, in fact, in all ages) the one who has kept in check the implementation of Satan's schemes and the effect of his multifarious activities is none other than the Holy Spirit. No other could possibly prevent the full outbreak of iniquity and the manifestation of the devil's masterpiece in "the man of sin."

The Holy Spirit indwells the church and also every individual believer. When the church is "translated" at our Lord's coming to the air, the Holy Spirit will cease to indwell individuals as at present and, in that sense, will be "taken out of the midst." Clearly He will continue to exercise His influence on humankind as He did previously, but the special relationship (John 14:16-17) that originated at Pentecost will never be repeated.

In His omnipresence, He will still be present in the world, but never as the
indweller of believers. As C. C. Ryrie said in *First and Second Thessalonians*, this is explained by "the difference of meaning between *residence*
and *presence*" (113).

If the Holy Spirit is the restrainer referred to in 2:7, it is evident that the
restricting influence in 2:6 can only be the church that He indwells.
Believers were regarded by our Lord as the salt of the earth and, while
they are present on earth, their influence prevents the complete corruption of human society. At the rapture, they will be removed and the Holy
Spirit will never indwell others in a similar fashion.

Doom of the Lawless

*Then will be revealed the lawless one, whom the Lord Jesus will
slay with the breath of His mouth and bring to naught with the
manifestation of His coming; even he, whose coming is according
to the working of Satan with all power and signs and wonders of
falsehood, and in all deceit of unrighteousness for those who are
perishing; because they received not the love of the truth that they
might be saved (2:8-10).*

With the removal of the restraints, the devil will be free to produce the
personal embodiment of lawlessness. Three times the apostle alluded to
the revelation of this man (vv. 3, 6, and 8). Findlay noted that there was a
suggestion of "some unearthly and portentous object, that holds the gazer
spellbound." Whether or not some miraculous event will attend his manifestation is not stated, but it is conceivable that, just as the birth of our
Lord was heralded by a star, so the appearance of this personage may be
accompanied by some remarkable sign. This may be the implication of
the words of 2:9.

The apostle also foretold the manner of termination of the brief career
of this evil character. The Lord Jesus will slay him with the breath of His
mouth. Centuries earlier, the prophet Isaiah predicted that, at the coming
of the messiah to introduce the golden age on earth, He would slay the
wicked with the breath of His lips (Isaiah 11:4). The Jewish exegetes
applied this to the destruction of an evil power to whom they accorded
the name of Armillus. Paul made clear the true identification and confirmed that the destruction will occur at our Lord's coming, His epiphany,
when He is manifested in glory to an adoring world. Then He will bring to

naught the one who personifies human defiance of God (see Revelation 19:20).

The advent of the lawless one, by contrast with the epiphany of the Lord Jesus, will be by the energizing of Satan, who will daringly introduce him with the same kind of signs as those attendant upon our Lord's ministry—power and signs and wonders—although they will all be false. As one writer said:

> With studied emphasis and precision Paul borrows for the coming of Antichrist the terms proper to the coming of Christ, making the one appear as a frightful mimicry and mocking prelude of the other. The lawless one has his "mystery," his "revelation," his "parousia," and his "power and signs and wonders," in which the "working of Satan" in him apes the working of God in Christ. This systematic and calculated adoption by Antichrist of the attributes of Christ is a most appalling feature in the apostle's representation. Satan himself, through his agent, usurps God's throne amongst men. And the man of lawlessness holds a relation towards Satan [which is] the counterpart of the relation of Christ to God.

The "working" here used of Satan is used elsewhere in the New Testament only of God, again emphasizing the diabolical imitation of the almighty.

The subjective aspect of the activities of Satan and his chosen one is indicated in 2:10. All deceit of unrighteousness or all unrighteous deceitfulness (either term is acceptable) would be employed for the seduction of mankind. Directed primarily against "those who are perishing," it will serve to seal their doom. They had the opportunity of receiving the truth, but the love of the truth had no appeal to their reprobate minds. When the final deceiver came with his convincing signs, they were completely lost.

The picture relates, of course, to the future, but we see many similar pictures in our present day. Those of whom the apostle wrote prophetically will succumb to the deceptions of the lawless one and inevitably plunge into perdition. They refused to receive the truth that would have brought salvation.

Delusion

And for this cause God sends them a working of error, so that they should believe the lie, that they all should be judged who did not believe the truth, but took pleasure in unrighteousness (2:11-12).

In portraying the evils of heathendom in his epistle to the Romans, the apostle Paul declared that, because of the corrupt practices of paganism and because of humankind's refusal to acknowledge and glorify God, God gave them up to uncleanness, vile passions, and a reprobate mind (Romans 1:24,26,28). It was a fitting punishment. As has been said, "God makes sin work out its own punishment." Persistent rejection of morality and righteousness destroys the consciousness of them and inevitably leads to immorality and unrighteousness.

So the willful rejection of truth leads to acceptance of the satanic delusion. God does not remain a passive spectator of evil. As the supreme judge, He is responsible for the punishment of sin. His judgment is never capricious or unreasonable, but completely just and equitable. Since the dupes of the lawless one had accepted the working of Satan, He would send on them a working of error, or delusion. He does not send error, but the inward working which results in the inescapable consequences of the error to which they had surrendered.

The delusion sent on them would result in their believing the lie, not merely falsehood in general but the claim of the lawless one to be divine (see also Revelation 13:15). This would be their crowning folly, the acme of evil, in that it involved unreserved rejection of God and of everything associated with Him. If they refused the truth, they would be thrust into the arms of error, compelled to reap the harvest of their sin.

They did not believe the truth but had pleasure in unrighteousness; in rejecting the truth, they automatically embraced falsehood. Their sin was both negative and positive. The divine purpose was that all such should be judged, with the implication that the verdict pronounced would be adverse. It has been suggested that there is a difference between this judgment and the final assize. Although our Lord will certainly judge those on earth who are alive at the time of His second advent (Matthew 25:32), the later judgment of the great white throne could only confirm that of a thousand years earlier.

12

The Antichrist

Writing near the end of the first century, the apostle John declared, "It is the last time, and as you have heard that antichrist will come, so now there are many antichrists; therefore you know that it is the last time" (1 John 2:18). And again, "Every spirit which does not confess that Jesus Christ has come in the flesh is not of God. This is the spirit of antichrist, of which you heard that it was coming, and now it is in the world already" (1 John 4:3). Although the concept is found elsewhere, John is the only biblical writer to use the term *antichrist*.

It is significant that he alluded not only to a person or persons, but also to a "spirit." He stated plainly that a denial of fundamental doctrine of the incarnation of Jesus Christ was "the spirit of antichrist," which was already in the world. This, and his earlier statement that even in his day there were many antichrists in existence, made it clear that although he doubtless envisaged the ultimate antichrist as a single person he also used the term to signify an evil power influencing others to disbelief. As William Barclay said in *The Letters of John and Jude*: "Just as the Holy Spirit was inspiring the true teachers and the true prophets, so there was an evil spirit inspiring the false teachers and the false prophets. . . . The spirit of antichrist was struggling with the Spirit of God for the possession of men's minds. . . . He no longer thought in terms of a single demonic figure but in terms of a force of evil deliberately seeking to pervade men's minds" (64).

"The teachers against whom" John warned his readers "were so many lesser antichrists who presumably were paving the way for the final antichrist himself. It is a reasonable inference from his language that the final antichrist would head a large-scale departure from God." John was fully aware that at the last time the ultimate antichrist would appear; he reminded his readers that they also were cognizant of this fact. Yet, paradoxically, when he wrote the apocalypse a few years later, while furnishing a vast amount of information about the future, he refrained (under the guidance of the Holy Spirit) from identifying this important character of the future.

F. F. Bruce said unhesitatingly that "the personage called 'the man of lawlessness' is certainly identical with the personage elsewhere referred to as Antichrist" (179), and there is little doubt that the apostle Paul intended this identification. Like the apostle John, he was fully acquainted with Jewish teaching on the subject, as was evidenced by his quotation from Isaiah 11:4 in his account of the end of the man of lawlessness (2 Thessalonians 2:8).

Apart altogether from the teaching based on the Old Testament, the concept of an evil power opposed to God had been prevalent from early in history, as for example in the Babylonian legend of creation. To quote Barclay:

> According to it, there was in the very beginning a primeval sea monster called Tiamat; this sea monster was subdued by Marduk but not killed; it was only asleep and the final battle was still to come. That mythical idea of the primeval monster occurs in the Old Testament again and again. There the monster is often called Rahab or the crooked serpent or leviathan. "Thou didst crush Rahab like a carcass," says the Psalmist (Psalm 89:10). "His hand pierced the fleeing serpent," says Job (Job 26:13). Isaiah, speaking of the arm of the Lord, says, "Was it not thou that didst cut Rahab in pieces, that didst pierce the dragon?" (Isaiah 51:9). Isaiah also writes, "In that day the Lord with his hand and great strong sword will punish leviathan the fleeing serpent, leviathan the twisting serpent, and he will slay the dragon that is in the sea" (Isaiah 27:1). All these are references to the primeval dragon. . . . In the universe there is a power hostile to God (61-62).

Although the Babylonian myth obviously affected the conception formed by many, the biblical revelation both preceded it (and was possibly reflected in it, rather than vice versa) and identified the serpent as Satan.

In rabbinical teaching, the power of evil became personalized and as Findlay said:

> In later Judaism, Antichrist was known as Armillus (or Armalgus), under which name he figures largely in the Jewish fables of the Middle Ages, the rabbinical conception being developed in forms partly analogous and partly hostile to the Christian doctrine. Armillus appears already in the *Targum of Jonathan* upon Isaiah 11:4, the passage [alluded to in 2 Thessalonians 2:8]: "With the breath of His lips shall He (the Messiah) slay Armillus, the wicked one." This interpretation was traditional, and may have been older than Christianity (172).

(It is commonly concluded today that it was, in fact, very much older). The apostle Paul was surely aware of what was taught by other religious teachers and philosophers.

On many occasions over the centuries, individuals have been regarded either as antichrist or as his precursor. For example, two centuries before the apostle wrote, Antiochus IV of Syria attracted the hatred of the Jews for placing the altar of the Olympian Zeus on the altar of Jehovah at Jerusalem, establishing the worship of the supreme heathen deity there. That sacrilegious action in 167 B.C. was so abhorrent to the Jews that they applied to it the description given four hundred years before by Daniel to the future self-deification of antichrist (Daniel 9:27). Daniel called it "the abomination of desolation" (see 1 Maccabees 1:54). Their removal of the desecrating object and the restoration of the temple are still celebrated in the festival of Hanukkah or Dedication.

In A.D. 40 similar emotions were aroused and the same terms of opprobrium employed when the Roman emperor Gaius (or Caligula) decided to set up a statue of himself for worship in the temple at Jerusalem. As things turned out, however, his blasphemous intention was never implemented.

By his interpretation of the abomination of desolation as a man standing "where he ought not" (Mark 13:14) and as an object standing "in the holy place" (Matthew 24:15), our Lord gave clearer shape to the somewhat nebulous Jewish conception. His words were recalled by many in A.D. 70

at the destruction of the temple and the presence of Roman standards in the temple court, although the application to those events was obviously inappropriate.

In the early church it was widely assumed that the man of sin could be no other than the emperor Nero, whose vices marked him out as a consummately evil character. When he died there was initially a reluctance to accept the report of his death, but the belief subsequently spread that he would one day reappear to fill the role of antichrist. The myth of a Nero redivivus circulated for a long time. *The Ascension of Isaiah*, an early Christian work, anticipated that antichrist would be the incarnation of Beliar (or Belial), the spirit of evil, and that he was identifiable with a revived Nero. Some of the *Sybilline Oracles* also refer to the return of Nero and to the future of Beliar.

The Nero legend died slowly (there are, in fact, still some who maintain that Revelation 13:3 can be fulfilled only by the resurrection of Nero). It was replaced by the theory that the term *antichrist* should be applied to the entire line of Roman emperors, particularly in view of their claim to divinity, but that theory ceased at the fall of the empire. The traditional association of antichrist with Rome, coupled with the papal claim to political sovereignty as well as ecclesiastical authority, almost inevitably led to the presumption that the pope was to be identified as the antichrist. Martin Luther maintained that the papal system, headed by the pope, was the antichrist and would be destroyed by Christ at His coming. Even as recently as 1646 the Westminster Confession of Faith stated, "There is no other head of the Church but the Lord Jesus Christ; nor can the Pope of Rome in any sense be the head thereof, but is that Antichrist, that man of sin and son of perdition, that exalteth himself in the Church against Christ and all that is called God."

But, as one writer emphasized, antichrist "is not an abstract power or collective concept, but definitely an eschatological person." The apostle Paul made clear that antichrist belongs to the endtime (2 Thessalonians 2:8).

It is natural that over the centuries outstanding individuals have appeared whose characteristics have seemed to reflect the biblical description of antichrist, and that they should consequently have been regarded as the man so long expected. Napoleon Bonaparte, for example, was long deemed to be probably the predicted antichrist. As Findlay said, "The empire of Napoleon was essentially a restoration of the military Caesarism of the first century. He came within a little of making himself, like

Julius Caesar, dictator of the civilized world" (178). He was undoubtedly
"in the true succession of Antiochus Epiphanes and Nero Caesar."

In the seventh century the identification of Muhammad as antichrist
found strong support. Other religious leaders have also been designated
as possibilities, but there has been a general tendency to turn to the
political realm for possible candidates. In comparatively recent years
Benito Mussolini, Adolf Hitler, Joseph Stalin, and others have at various
times been named as possibly filling the role. By the use of *gematria*, the
number 666 (Revelation 13:18), by which the beast will be identifiable in
a future day, has been ingeniously employed to prove that quite a number
of contemporary individuals may be the expected antichrist.

From time to time, circumstances arise that seem comparable to those
expected to apply at the endtime. It is significant that on each such
occasion there usually exists a prominent individual who might conceivably fill the role of the long-anticipated antichrist. With his knowledge of
the course of events in the past and also of the biblical revelation of the
divine program, Satan has almost undoubtedly set his mark on a suitable
man on each of these occasions in preparation for the expected events.
There has unquestionably been a long line of precursors—any one of
whom might have been the devil's choice had the appointed hour
struck—who will eventually be succeeded by the final man of lawlessness in whom there will be the full revelation of satanic power and
hostility to God.

In *The Antichrist Legend* W. Bousset traced the development of the
doctrine of antichrist and outlined the features that he concluded were
generally accepted. F. F. Bruce ably summarized his account:

> According to Bousset's reconstruction of the Antichrist expectation,
> Antichrist would appear among the Jews after the fall of Rome,
> proclaiming his divine status and installing his cult in the Jerusalem
> temple. He would himself be a Jew, born of the tribe of Dan (an idea
> based on Genesis 49:17; Deuteronomy 33:22; Jeremiah 8:16). Elijah
> would appear and denounce him, and would be put to death for his
> pains. Antichrist would reign for three and a half years. True believ-
> ers, refusing to give him the worship he demanded, would seek
> refuge in the wilderness and be pursued by him there but when they
> are on the point of being wiped out, he is destroyed by the interven-
> tion of God (who may use an angel such as Michael the archangel
> or the Messiah of David's line) (179).

The student of prophecy will probably not accept every detail of the picture presented, but it does conform broadly with the biblical revelation.

Daniel predicted (Daniel 9:24-27) that a period of seventy heptads or 490 years would run from the date of an instruction to rebuild Jerusalem (see Nehemiah 2:4-8). It is clear from Daniel 9:26 that there was a break in the continuity of the period after the 483rd year and that the events of Daniel 9:27 relate to the end time. (It is logical to conclude that the parenthesis, which has lasted for nearly two thousand years, has been filled with the present church era.) According to the prophet, after the lapse of half of the last seven years, all religious worship would be proscribed and there would ensue the "abomination of desolation" (or the desolating idolatry).

As already mentioned, in His Olivet discourse our Lord indicated that the abomination of desolation was associated with the temple at Jerusalem and would take the form of an object and a person. In Revelation 13:1-8; 17:10-14, John disclosed that out of the gentile nations a great power would arise who would have dominion over ten nations (cf. Daniel 2:41-43; 7:23-25) and whose rule would continue for three-and-a-half years (Revelation 13:5; cf. Daniel 7:25). In honor of this supreme ruler a statue would be made, to which life would be imparted, and all would be commanded to worship the statue on penalty of death. The statue is presumably that to which our Lord referred (Matthew 24:15). The apostle Paul declared that the man of lawlessness (evidently identifiable with the great ruler described by John) will sit in the temple, claiming homage as God (2 Thessalonians 2:3-4), doubtless the person referred to by the master (Mark 13:14). In confirmation of Paul's words to the Thessalonians John portrayed the destruction of this man, the final antichrist, at the second advent of Christ in all His glory (Revelation 19:20).

The day of the Lord will commence at the manifestation of this man (2 Thessalonians 2:3), but that period of judgment has no relevance to the Christian (1 Thessalonians 5:1-9). Our Lord refers to the same period as the great tribulation and declares that it will commence with the manifestation of this man, described symbolically as the abomination of desolation and will conclude with the second advent (Matthew 24:21,29), i.e., His return to earth as deliverer of Israel and universal sovereign (Zechariah 14:4,9), which is distinct from His coming to the air to remove His church (John 14:3; 1 Thessalonians 4:16-17) and to preserve His people from the hour of the tribulation (Revelation 3:10).

The appearance of antichrist is clearly to occur midway through the last seven years of Daniel 9:27; in other words, during a period when time is once more being reckoned. Time has no relevance to heaven or to God's heavenly people Israel. There is, for example, no indication of the duration of the church era, nor the date of any events that might occur during that period. As Daniel 9:26 implies, the biblical reckoning of time ceased at the crucifixion and will not recommence until the negotiation of the treaty referred to in Daniel 9:27.

A parenthesis of nearly two thousand years has elapsed since the cross, during which the Holy Spirit has been adding men and women to the church. It is logical to conclude that the termination of the church era by the "translation" of the church from earth will be the signal for the recommencement of time-reckoning. It follows, therefore, that the appearance of antichrist will not be witnessed by any Christians on earth, since it will not take place for at least three-and-a-half years after the rapture of the church. He cannot appear while the church is on earth. Consequently all present attempts to identify him must fail.

13

Comfort and Encouragement

2 Thessalonians 2:13–3:5

It is perhaps only natural that the didactic section of 2 Thessalonians should attract considerable attention because of its eschatological content. That matter is indeed of such serious and important character that the value of the hortatory section tends to be underestimated.

Thanksgiving

Now we are bound to give thanks to God always for you, brethren, beloved of the Lord, because God chose you from the beginning to salvation in sanctification of the Spirit and belief in the truth; to which end He called you through our gospel, that you might obtain the glory of our Lord Jesus Christ. So then, brethren, stand fast, and hold the traditions which you were taught, whether by word or our epistle (2:13-15).

With minor variations, Paul repeated the opening words of thanksgiving in chapter 1:3 of this epistle, making clear that the doctrinal instruction had been concluded and the original thanksgiving and train of thought had resumed. The missionaries felt it their duty constantly to give thanks to God for their Thessalonian converts, described as "beloved of the Lord." In 2:8 our Lord had been portrayed as the destroyer of the evil personage, the lawless one. The same Lord had set His heart's affection on these believers.

Thanks were due to God because He chose the Thessalonians to salvation from the beginning. Their salvation owed nothing to themselves or their inclinations; it resulted entirely from the divine initiative. They had been marked out beforehand by divine election, which, as the aorist indicative makes plain, occurred at a specific moment in the past. The AV and some other versions indicate that the choice was made "from the beginning," and some have interpreted this as the time of the preaching in Thessalonica. But as Hogg and Vine stated, "Paul does not elsewhere speak of the election of men unto salvation taking place in time; what takes place in time is God's call" (271). "The beginning" must be interpreted as in the eternity of the past. It was then that God made His choice.

On the other hand, some ground exists for translating "as firstfruits" instead of "from the beginning." James later referred to believers as firstfruits of creation (James 1:18), and John described others of a future day as the firstfruits of mankind (Revelation 14:4). In the Jewish economy a sheaf of the firstfruits of the harvest was always presented to God as a wave offering (Leviticus 23:19-20). It is possible that the apostle had in mind the Old Testament symbolism in his description of the Thessalonians, regarding them as a kind of firstfruits of the multitudes who would later be gathered out of the world. But it is more logical to interpret his words as intimating that the choice of these believers had preceded time, having occurred in the ageless past.

The salvation to be experienced was not restricted to their release from the fetters of sin. It anticipated the eventual possession of the glory of Christ (2:14), effected in sanctification by the Spirit and belief in the truth. The omission of the article may imply that it was their spirits which were being sanctified; if the Holy Spirit was intended, then the sanctification as a process was being effected by His power. Since their belief of the truth arose from a personal exercise of faith, the emphasis was probably on their spirit rather than on the Holy Spirit.

With a view to the realization of His purpose, God called them through the gospel preached by the apostolic band. It was by such means that the Thessalonians became aware of the purposes of God; by their response to the evangelistic appeal, it became practicable for the divine intentions to be implemented.

Their salvation involved not only their belief of the truth (or their acceptance of the truth of the gospel) and their continuing sanctification by the Holy Spirit, but also their ultimate obtaining of the glory of our Lord Jesus Christ. They were not immediately translated to heaven, but the culmination of their salvation would be in the sharing of the Lord's glory in the day of His exaltation.

In view of all that had been said, the apostle enjoined them to stand fast or to be steadfast. He had begged them not to be shaken or loosed from their moorings (2:2); now he desired them to take a firm grip on the traditions they had been taught, whether orally or by letter. He had grounded them in the faith and had committed to them the body of Christian doctrine, which they were to hold unwaveringly and tenaciously. These teachings were not of human origin, but rather the revelation of the mind and purposes of God. Paul's charge is still applicable in essence today.

Divine Encouragement

Now our Lord Jesus Christ Himself and God our Father, who has loved us and has given us eternal encouragement and good hope through grace, comfort your hearts and establish them in every good work and word (2:16-17).

From exhortation Paul turned to what has been termed another wish-prayer (cf. 1 Thessalonians 3:11-13 and 5:23). It is interesting that he named the Lord Jesus Christ before God the Father, although he normally used the reverse order, the reason possibly being the prominence given to the Lord in the preceding paragraph. But the order does indicate that in the apostle's mind there was equality between the Son and the Father. Indeed, the construction of the entire prayer and the use of singular verbs may well have been intended to emphasize the unity of the persons in the godhead.

Not only had the Thessalonians been recipients of divine love, but had been given "eternal encouragement" (or comfort), the provision of courage in the face of their present distress and tribulation and also for their future path. "Good hope," not only as the blessings of a future eternity with Christ, but as a present possession, had also been bestowed on them. They could rise above the depressing circumstances of daily experience to revel in a greater realm of bliss and joy. These gifts had been given to them by divine grace—not on the basis of any personal merit.

The apostle uttered two specific petitions. First, he sought that the Lord and the Father might comfort or encourage their hearts. Only divine comfort could allay fear and uncertainty.

Second, he prayed that God would establish them in every good work and word (not "word and work" as in the AV). This was a reversal of Paul's usual order (Romans 15:18; 2 Corinthians 10:11; Colossians 3:17), where precept was regarded as preceding practice. It has been suggested that the order indicated a recognition of the spiritual maturity of the readers, but that idea seems rather far-fetched. Because the Thessalonians had demonstrated their faith and love by their works, the order may have been a subtle commendation of their practical Christian living.

Prayer and Progress

For the rest, brethren, pray for us, that the word of the Lord may run and be glorified, even as it has with you; and that we may be delivered from perverse and evil men; for not all have faith (3:1-2).

As in the first epistle (1 Thessalonians 5:25) the apostle repeated his request for the prayers of the Thessalonian brethren. "His word runs very swiftly," the psalmist had written long before (Psalm 147:15), and Paul now sought fellowship in prayer that "the word of the Lord may run and be glorified," thus applying psalmist's words to the progress of the gospel. He pictured the glad evangel sweeping triumphantly to success, thereby bringing blessing. Since the word had sounded forth from these Thessalonian believers into all the neighboring region, the apostle desired their prayers that the same irresistible force might sweep in blessing through Achaia also.

He also desired their prayers that the missionaries might be delivered from perverse and evil men. The term *perverse* might equally well be rendered "outrageous." The Thessalonians were well aware of the Jewish antagonism in their own city and would doubtless know of similar opposition being experienced at Corinth. They could therefore pray intelligently for the protection of God's servants elsewhere.

The hostility of those referred to was because of their unbelief. They had no faith in the gospel and developed a hatred for it and its messengers. "Not all have faith"—an understatement of the case. The gospel always produces both negative and positive reactions.

Divine Faithfulness

But the Lord is faithful, who will establish you and guard you from the evil one. And we have confidence in the Lord concerning you

*that you both do and will do the things which we charge. Now may
the Lord direct your hearts into the love of God and into the patience of Christ (3:3-5).*

From the depressing lack of faith on the part of perverse men, the apostle
made a happy transition to the faithfulness of Christ. In contrast to the
untrustworthiness of men, he emphasized the complete reliability of
the Lord. The structure of the sentences made clear that he intended the
stressing of the contrast. The two relevant words were brought into close
juxtaposition: "not all have *faith*. But *faithful* is the Lord" (faith and
faithfulness are virtually the same word in Greek). The frailty of sinful and
rebellious man was thrown into the shadows by the infinite dependability
of the master Himself. Paul's normal expression "God is faithful" is
amended here to "the Lord is faithful," because he had been stressing the
second person of the godhead in these two epistles.

The one who was faithful would also establish them. In view of the
excitement and instability existing among the believers, particularly because of the eschatological controversy and the current persecution, their
greatest spiritual need was for a settled steady confidence. It was just this
that the Lord would give them.

Moreover, He would guard them from the evil one (not merely from evil
in general), a reflection of the petition in the Lord's prayer (Matthew 6:13).
As other of his epistles make clear, Paul was not ignorant of the power of
Satan and his followers. He realized the way in which the devil might
employ the bitter antagonism of the human enemies of these Thessalonians. He was well aware of the incessant attacks on God's people that
derived from the activity of hostile spirit forces. As Findlay remarked, "The
conflict of the church and of the Christian life is not a matter of principles
alone and abstract forces; it is a personal encounter, and behind all
forces there are living wills." The word *guard* is a military term, implying
armed protection in military conflict. A battle was being conducted by
unseen powers, but the protection of the omnipotent Lord was sufficient
for His people.

In the closing days of the church era in which we live, satanic opposition is greater than ever before. Aware that his time is short, Satan's efforts
to frustrate God's purposes and to destroy the witness of the children of
God are being intensified. His activities and influence should never be
underestimated. But it is still true that God will guard His people from all
the insidious attacks and malicious machinations of the evil one.

The apostle then expressed his confidence in the Lord that the Thessalonian converts would continue to put into practice the apostolic injunctions, not only those given in the course of teaching during the campaign at Thessalonica, but particularly those contained in this letter to the church there. Paul's words here may have had special relevance to the exhortations and admonitions contained in the remainder of 2 Thessalonians 3, including those about the indolent and disorderly. There was also an implicit commendation in the words; the apostle expressed his satisfaction with their obedience to the teaching of the missionaries by his reference to the believers' already doing the things they had been charged to do.

Then Paul once more voiced a spontaneous prayer, asking for their deeper experiential appreciation of God's love and their greater participation in the endurance of Christ. Fuller comprehension of the vastness and wealth of God's love could result only in a willing reciprocation of that love. Only an understanding of that love would provide motivation for obedience to the divine will as presented in the apostolic teaching.

The AV renders the last clause "into the patient waiting for Christ," restricting the concept to the Christian's waiting for the return of his Lord. W. F. Adeney considered that this is in harmony with the fact that "the dominant theme of both epistles is the second coming of Christ. . . . They should learn patience in waiting for the great consummation. The chief purposes of this epistle is to inculcate patience with that end in view" (251). If this view is adopted, the prayer was that in spite of the fires of persecution which they were experiencing they should, in steadfast endurance, be waiting for the return of their Lord.

But, as the RV and other versions make clear, the patience is not that of the believers but of their Lord. The patience of Christ is illustrated repeatedly in the gospel narratives. It is exemplified also in His patient waiting for the moment of His manifestation and vindication, as well as for the earlier union with His blood-bought bride. The attitude of the master should become the characteristic of the servant. They knew the certainty of the divine promises and could therefore wait in quiet expectation for their fulfillment.

There was undoubtedly an emphasis on the reproduction of the characteristics of Christ in the lives of His followers. If their hearts (their affections and motivations) were directed into the channels indicated, the beauty of Christ would obviously be seen again in His people.

14

Final Exhortations

2 Thessalonians 3:6-18

The letters of the apostle Paul were never purely doctrinal in content, although they were normally written to explain some doctrinal subject, to refute some heresy, or to reply to queries on points of teaching or practical matters. Having dealt with the doctrinal instruction needed, it was Paul's usual custom to conclude a letter with an admonition on Christian living, exhortations on practical details, or encouragement for life's road. The final section of 2 Thessalonians is of this character.

It was concerned primarily with those whom he regarded as disorderly in conduct and who were in need of discipline. Findlay's comments are pertinent. In 1 Thessalonians Paul

> had found it needful to exhort his readers to live a quiet life and to attend to their daily duties and pursuits. Some members of the church were of an idle and improvident disposition. The day of the Lord, they supposed, was imminent, and worldly occupations would, therefore, soon be at an end; the only business worth minding any longer, so they said, was to prepare for His coming. Their conduct was likely to bring discredit on the whole community; and they did it a material injury by throwing the burden of their maintenance on their hard-working and charitable brethren. These men

were "the disorderly" of 1 Thessalonians 5:12-14; they gave trouble to the officers of the church, whom the apostle in the first epistle urges the Thessalonians loyally to support, while they united to "admonish" the offenders. This evil, which should have been checked by the reproofs of the first letter, had grown to larger proportions. The startling announcements that were made respecting the Second Advent tended to aggravate the mischief. Indeed, these rumours so unhinged the minds of some of the Thessalonian Christians, that it must have been difficult for them, however diligently inclined, to pursue their common avocations. And the apostle, having calmed the agitation of his readers by what he has written in the second chapter, proceeds now in strong terms to rebuke the disorder which had thus been unhappily fostered and stimulated (162).

The admonition given in the first epistle (5:14) had evidently been relatively ineffective. Those who were at fault persisted, as W. L. Lane said, "in the professional loafing which suited their disposition." Sterner and more peremptory methods were obviously essential if the disorder was to be checked.

Discipline

Now we charge you, brethren, in the name of our Lord Jesus Christ, that you withdraw yourselves from every brother walking disorderly and not after the tradition which they received from us (3:6).

The unruliness and the disinclination to follow the apostolic injunctions demanded that disciplinary action should be taken. Affectionately yet authoritatively, the apostle made a solemn charge to the sober majority of the church. The charge was uttered as a judicial sentence in the name of the Lord Jesus Christ. Final authority lay with the Lord, but Paul was acting as judge in His name. There was no argument and there could be no appeal.

He directed the members of the church to withdraw from those who had brought discredit on the church by their idle and undisciplined lives. This was evidently not tantamount to formal excommunication or expulsion from the church, but rather a complete dissociation from those who were the cause of the action. The orderly believers were to keep aloof from every Christian who was not prepared to work for his living. The segregation of the indolent and the refusal to have fellowship with them should impress on such individuals the impropriety of their conduct.

The behavior of these men was also described negatively as "not after the tradition which they received from" the apostolic band. The missionaries had obviously given clear oral instruction on practical Christian living, and the contents of the first epistle had supplied further teaching. The idlers of the Thessalonian church had not merely neglected the teaching but had deliberately ignored it and were therefore to be shunned.

Today even some professing Christians find it preferable to rely exclusively on public assistance when they could work, saying quite plainly that it is financially better not to work. That is not a Christian attitude, but one condemned by the apostle.

Example

You know of yourselves how you ought to imitate us; for we behaved not ourselves disorderly among you; neither did we eat anyone's bread for nothing, but worked with labour and toil night and day, that we might not burden any of you. Not because we have not the right, but to furnish you with an example in ourselves, so that you might imitate us (3:7-9).

Jewish fathers always made sure that their sons were taught a trade of some kind as a provision against poverty or indolence. Many sons of wealthy men consequently learned a craft. In his youth the apostle Paul had learned the craft of tentmaking, a rough task of an irksome character and poorly remunerated. He supported himself by his physical labors in this way, although gifts were occasionally sent to him by churches and individuals. In his farewell address to the Ephesian elders, he displayed his rough, coarsened hands, with their testimony of his labors, and said, "These hands have ministered to my necessities and to those who were with me" (Acts 20:34).

Paul had taught by practice as well as precept at Thessalonica. Now he plainly drew attention to his own example, telling his readers what they already knew: that they ought to imitate him. He had demonstrated in practice the principles of a Christian life. Laziness and sloth had no part in the lives of the missionary band, and their converts should follow the example that had been set before them. The apostle emphasized that the missionaries had not lived in a disorderly manner among the believers (the term *disorderly* was used of soldiers who were out of step or out of rank).

When our Lord sent forth the twelve disciples to preach, He explicitly told them not to carry additional clothing or equipment for their journeys, "For the workman is worthy of his food" (Matthew 10:10). The mosaic law laid down that an ox was not to be muzzled when it was treading out the corn (Deuteronomy 25:4); in other words, it was entitled to eat as a recompense for working. The apostle Paul used this quotation as evidence that he was entitled to practical support while laboring in the ministry (1 Corinthians 9:9). He referred to the same Old Testament principle to justify support for elders, particularly those devoted to the ministry and teaching (1 Timothy 5:18).

In spite of his right to receive support from those among whom he labored, he declared that while in Thessalonica the missionaries "did not eat anyone's bread for nothing." The reference was not merely to receiving food without payment; the words were a hebraic synonym for practical maintenance (2 Samuel 9:7). They had not been parasites, but had deliberately maintained themselves by manual labor. In fact, the apostle said quite bluntly that they had worked "with labour and toil night and day" in order not to burden any of their converts. In his first epistle he had reminded them plainly that the missionaries had worked night and day in order not to be indebted to any of the believers. Those facts were known to his readers and were in stark contrast to the attitude of certain lazy members of the church, who evidently expected to be supported materially, without working themselves.

No one could accuse these missionaries of preaching for financial gain; rather, their sacrificial labors were an implicit condemnation of the unworthy conduct of the shameless ones who were burdening the church and taxing their charity. For some reason, those individuals evidently considered that they were entitled to support, even if only for their meddlesome activities in the affairs of others (3:11).

Even if the missionaries had not availed themselves of any potential advantage, Paul asserted emphatically that it was not because they had no authority to do so. Their entitlement was clear, and financial gifts were, in fact, accepted by them from other churches. But here they had refrained from accepting maintenance of any kind, in order that their conduct might furnish an example for imitation by the Thessalonians (cf. Philippians 3:17).

Not only was there rebuke to the disorderly, but encouragement to the church in general to live in a fashion comparable to the example set them. By stressing the missionaries' right, even if not exercised, the apostle ensured that other workers should not be denied the privilege that he and his co-workers had denied themselves.

The Principle

For even when we were with you, this we used to charge you. If any will not work, neither let him eat. For we hear that there are some among you who are walking disorderly, who do not work at all, but are busybodies. Now those that are such, we charge and exhort in the Lord Jesus Christ that, working with quietness, they eat their own bread (3:10-12).

The undesirable tendencies now seen so plainly were evident to the missionaries when they first visited the city. Paul had obviously foreseen the probable development and, even during the short time the evangelists were at Thessalonica, they had enunciated the principle that if anyone refused to work, he should not eat (cf. Genesis 3:19). There was nothing demeaning in honest work and, if some were not prepared to accept the monotony of daily toil to earn a livelihood, their needs should not be met by others. No reproach was cast on those unable to work for some reason; the emphasis was on those who were unwilling to do so. As A. J. Mason said, "To any weakness or incapacity for work, except in himself, St. Paul would be very tender; the vice consists in the defective will." Some have seen in the principle laid down by the apostle a condemnation of the "idle rich," whose income is assured and who do not therefore need to engage in work. Even such, of course, have a responsibility to the world and to God to make some useful contribution to life. R. C. H. Lenski in *The Interpretation of St. Paul's Epistles* remarked that Paul's "dictum abolishes all false asceticism, all unchristian disinclination to work, all fanatic exaltation above work, all self-inflicted pauperism" (472). Deliberate loafing should not be subsidized by misguided charity.

The oral and written instructions were obviously necessary because the missionaries had learned that there were some in the church (doubtless known by name) who were like this. Findlay said, "Further news had come since Paul wrote the first epistle, in which he touched briefly, in mild and general terms, upon the subject (1 Thessalonians 4:11-12; 5:14).

Now he is compelled to single out the offenders and to address them with pointed censure." Their public conduct was a disgrace to the church.

Their discreditable behavior had a positive aspect as well as a negative. Using a play on words, the apostle said that their one business was to be busybodies. He had previously bidden all of them to "study to be quiet and to do their own work" (1 Thessalonians 4:11), but some still insisted on pursuing their meddlesome activities—and doing that presumably in addition to the disquiet they were creating by the propagation of their misleading eschatological views. Their particular activities are not indicated, but they were obviously disturbing other believers and affecting the honor of the church.

Paul solemnly charged these individuals in the Lord Jesus Christ (claiming Christ's authority for the command) that they should adopt an entirely different attitude. Instead of their restless, disturbing fussiness, they should adopt a calm tranquility and peacefulness and engage in consistent and regular employment to support themselves materially. Denying them, in effect, the right to impose on their fellow-Christians, he charged them to earn their own livelihood and to cease being a nuisance to others. W. Neil summed it up tersely as: "Stop fussing, stop idling, and stop sponging."

The Faithful

But as for you, brethren, be not weary in well-doing. But if anyone obeys not our word by this epistle, note that man, that you have no company with him, to the end that he may be ashamed. Yet do not regard him as an enemy, but admonish him as a brother (3:13-15).

In contrast to the unworthy characters in their midst, the faithful were exhorted to perseverance in well-doing (cf. Galatians 6:9). The constant need for disciplining the indolent and counseling them to tread a different path might well have dampened the ardor and enthusiasm of others, but it was not to this discouragement that the apostle alluded. He was probably concerned rather with the general weariness and loss of zeal that is always liable to occur after long and sustained effort. But he appealed to them not to slacken their efforts but to persist in doing good (not merely almsgiving, as some have suggested, but whatever is right and good).

The epistle would, no doubt, be read publicly to the assembled church; some of the disorderly would acknowledge their fault and accept the apostolic admonition. There was, however, the possibility that others, more refractory, would refuse to comply with the instructions given by Paul. The church was held responsible to discipline such persons. Indeed, if they did not, even more scandalous conditions might arise.

The apostle called on the faithful to mark any disobedient individual as one with whom they should not associate. The insubordination exhibited demonstrated the character of the man and, for his recalcitrance, he was to feel the church's disapproval. This did not mean full and formal excommunication, but rather social ostracism, a severance of fellowship with other Christians.

Such discipline was intended to have a remedial effect. The purpose was that he might be abashed or ashamed of his obstinate behavior. The aim of discipline should always be the restoration of the wrongdoer; the door for repentance must always be left wide open. Consequently, the apostle specifically enjoined his readers not to regard the erring one as an enemy to be hated and rejected, but instead as a brother for whom admonishment had become necessary. That person's disobedience demanded action, but not of such a nature as to cause a rupture in the church.

Conclusion

Now may the Lord of peace Himself give you peace at all times in all ways. The Lord be with you all. The salutation of me, Paul, with my own hand, which is the token in every epistle, thus I write. The grace of our Lord Jesus Christ be with you all (3:16-18).

The prayer that his readers might enjoy peace was frequently expressed in Paul's letters (e.g. Ephesians 6:23; Philippians 4:9) but his normal phraseology "the God of peace," became "the Lord of Peace" in this instance—the only use of this term. The Thessalonian church obviously needed peace. As Findlay said:

Peace was disturbed by an irritating kind of disorder in the church, by wild rumours and alarms respecting the parousia (2:1-2), as well as by the unrelenting persecution from without. St. Paul has done his best to tranquillize his readers' minds, and bring them all to a sober and orderly condition. But he looks to "the Lord of peace Himself" to shed on them his all-controlling and all-reconciling influence.

He is the source of peace and the only one who can fully establish peace. So Paul prayed to the Lord of peace to give them peace. He desired the continual and uninterrupted experience of that peace for them, "at all times in all ways." Nothing need disturb that deep experience (John 14:27).

"The Lord be with you all," he wrote. Only through the personal presence of the Lord in their midst would the desired peace be mediated to the church and every member of it. Here were both strength and comfort (Matthew 28:20).

The apostle usually employed one of his fellow-helpers as an amanuensis, but to authenticate this epistle he added the concluding sentences and his signature in his own writing. It had apparently been alleged that a letter from him made statements which he had never made (2 Thessalonians 2:2), and it was all the more necessary therefore that this epistle should be accepted as genuine (cf. 1 Corinthians 16:21; Galatians 6:11; Colossians 4:18). Paul stated that it was his practice in every epistle to add the salutation in his own writing and, by implication, that this was an attestation of the epistle. He did not, however, in every case, add his signature, as in this epistle.

The epistle concluded with the benediction, "The grace of our Lord Jesus Christ be with you all," the last word being especially significant in view of the censure he had passed on some members of the church. All were included in the benediction. The *amen* with which the AV concludes the epistle is absent from most manuscripts and seems to have been a scribal addition.

15

The Letters Still Speak

The timid pro-Jewish Claudius had been cajoled into repeating the action of Tiberius and ordering the expulsion of all Jews from Rome. Like many others, an exiled couple named Aquila and Priscilla made their way to the wealthy but dissolute city of Corinth to establish a new home there. Corinth was a walled town, standing under the shadow of the 2,000-foot high mountain of Acro-Corinth, on the summit of which stood the temple of Aphrodite, served by a thousand priestesses. The "streets thronged with merchants and industrialists, Romans, Greeks, Jews, Syrians and Egyptians, drawn together by the hope of money" (H. V. Morton). The city was notorious in the ancient world for both its prosperity and its vice.

Aquila and Priscilla were makers of tent cloth, or *cilicium*, and since the harbors of Cenchreae and Lechaeum were constantly crowded with ships, there was always ample work for their hands. To their house subsequently came the apostle Paul, who had been trained in the same craft. He was, as H. V. Morton wrote in *The Steps of St. Paul*,

> a man of middle age, hardened by years of travel and privation, the marks of the rods of the Philippian lictors still on his body, the memory of the Thessalonian persecution still in his mind, and in his ears the mocking laughter of the Athenian philosophers. . . . He did

118

not intend to stay long in Corinth. That is evident from verses 17 and 18 of chapter 2 of the First Epistle to the Thessalonians, which was written from Corinth. He came to the city, longing to go north again to Macedonia, waiting anxiously for Silas and Timothy to come, so that he could make plans to return with them and resume in Thessalonica the work which had been so violently interrupted by his Jewish enemies (301).

In the meantime, he worked to support himself, sitting daily with Aquila stitching sails to carry ships far and wide.

On the sabbath, needle and thread were laid aside and the Lord's servant preached Christ in the synagogue. As a result, a number of people were converted. Throughout the winter Paul worked and preached, and eventually in the spring Silas and Timothy arrived in Corinth to join their leader. They found him, said Morton,

> living as usual in an atmosphere of mental and spiritual energy, preaching with tremendous zeal, and his success had again stirred up the Jews against him. Their animosity culminated in a terrible scene. During an argument in the synagogue, the Jews cursed Christ. . . . Paul rose in anger and performed the symbolic gesture of repudiation (304).

He left the synagogue and turned to the gentiles. Close to the synagogue was the spacious house of a Roman colonist named Titus Justus, and the converts followed the apostle there. This apparently became his headquarters (Acts 18:1-7). It may well have been from here that he dictated his two epistles to the Thessalonians. He remained in Corinth for eighteen months, still unable to return to Thessalonica to see his beloved converts.

Paul's enforced separation from the believers at Thessalonica and his inability to return to them to complete the teaching he had given them have paradoxically been the source of inestimable blessing to the Christian church. The direct consequence was the two unique letters that he addressed to them. His epistles to other churches were concerned with particular doctrines, statements of faith, refutation of heresy, or correction of error in belief or practice. In the Thessalonians letters the references to such subjects were almost incidental. It is true that he gave instructions on practical sanctification—moral conduct, discipline, slothfulness, idleness—but these were not his primary objects in writing.

An interesting feature is the revelation the epistles give of the writer himself. As F. F. Bruce remarked in *The New Bible Commentary*,

> Paul reveals himself in every sentence as a true and faithful pastor, rejoicing in his flock but anxious for their welfare, confident and concerned, thanking God for them and simultaneously praying to God for them as a father for his children, straining his strength to the limit in order not to be a burden to them (1053).

To quote C. A. A. Scott:

> Here was a new phenomenon in history, a man to whom the religious steadfastness and ethical progress of other men was a matter of life and death (see especially 1 Thessalonians 2:8,9; 3:6-8).

His deep love for the Thessalonian converts is evident in the letters.

The epistles also throw considerable light on the apostle's personal experiences at the hands of those who opposed his preaching of Christ. The attempts to undermine his authority, to discredit his motives, to denigrate his character, to malign his intentions, and to misinterpret his teaching—all clearly implied in the letters—must have affected his sensitive spirit and caused him considerable grief. But any effort he made at vindication was concerned primarily with the authority divinely bestowed on him and the ministry to which he had been divinely called.

The value of the epistles for the present day lies largely in their eschatological teaching. During his brief residence at Thessalonica, the apostle obviously covered a wide range of teaching on the subject of prophecy; one of the major reasons for the epistles was to deal with problems arising out of what had been taught.

The first matter was the impropriety of abandoning all normal work and activities because of the belief that our Lord's return was so imminent that it was pointless to pursue regular life. That belief had inevitably led to indolence and slothfulness, and the apostle justifiably condemned such conduct and reprimanded those who refused to work. The "blessed hope" should be an inspiration and incentive, not a brake.

A second problem related to the prospect of Christians who had already died. The concern of their surviving friends elicited the revelation that those who had died would be the first to receive their new bodies, but that when that occurs (at Christ's descent to the air) living believers would also be caught up with them to meet the Lord in the air. Every member of Christ's mystical body, the church, will be at that tremendous reunion.

A third difficulty arose from a misunderstanding about the day of the Lord. The apostle showed that it had no relevance to the Christian, and that the coming of that period of judgment cannot occur until the removal of certain hindrances. When that happens, apostasy will culminate in the manifestation of the antichrist.

The Thessalonian letters will always have an appeal for average Christians, if only for the comfort and strength furnished by the apostle's words in 1 Thessalonians 4:13-18. How many grieving hearts have been lifted up by the reminder that the Christian does not sorrow like those without hope, that our departed loved ones are not only safe but that one day they will be reunited with us. How many an aged pilgrim, weary with the journey of life, has lifted up his head at the thought of the Lord's coming. Here is the blessed hope. Here is the inspiration to live and work for the master. Carl F. H. Henry aptly said, "Hope in the future lends such a meaning to life that even where the Christian revelation is unknown, men and women dream of some new era of promise."

The Christian's hope is certain and assured of fulfillment. It is centered in a person. Whatever other message the Thessalonian letters convey, they declare that Christ is surely coming.

Recommended Readings

Bailey, J. W. 1955. *The First and Second Epistles to the Thessalonians*. Nashville: Abingdon Press.

Best, E. 1972. *The First and Second Epistles to the Thessalonians*. New York: Harper Brothers.

Bicknell, E. J. 1933. *The First and Second Epistles to the Thessalonians*. London: Methuen.

Bousset, W. B. 1896. *The Antichrist Legend*. London: Hutchinson.

Bruce, F. F. 1982. *1 and 2 Thessalonians*. Waco: Word Books.

Darby, J. N. 1869. *Notes on the Epistles to the Thessalonians*. London: C. A. Hammond.

Denney, J. 1872. *The Epistles to the Thessalonians*. London: Hodder and Stoughton Ltd.

Ellicott, C. J. 1844. *A Critical and Grammatical Commentary on St. Paul's Epistles to the Thessalonians*. Andover: Warren F. Draper.

English, E. S. 1954. *The Rapture*. Neptune NJ: Loizeaux Brothers, Inc.

Erdman, C. R. 1935. *The Epistles of Paul to the Thessalonians*. Philadelphia: Westminster Press.

Findlay, G. G. 1911. *The Epistles of Paul the Apostle to the Thessalonians*. Cambridge: Cambridge University Press.

———. 1898. *The Epistles to the Thessalonians*. Cambridge: Cambridge University Press.

Frame, J. E. 1912. *The Epistles of St. Paul to the Thessalonians*. Edinburgh: T. & T. Clark.

———. 1912. *A Critical and Exegetical Commentary on the Epistles of St. Paul to the Thessalonians*. New York: Charles Scribner's Sons.

Hendrikson, W. 1972. *I and II Thessalonians*. London: Banner of Truth.

Hiebert, D. E. 1977. *The Thessalonian Epistles*. Chicago: Moody Press.

Hogg, C. F. and W. E. Vine. 1916. *The Epistles of Paul the Apostle to the Thessalonians*. Glasgow: Pickering & Inglis Ltd.

Horne, C. M. 1961. *The Epistles to the Thessalonians*. Grand Rapids MI: Baker Book House.

Hubbard, D. A. 1977. *Thessalonians*. Waco: World Books.

Kelly, W. 1913. *The Epistles of Paul the Apostle to the Thessalonians*. London: C. A. Hammond.

Marshall, I. H. 1983. *1 and 2 Thessalonians*. Grand Rapids MI: Wm. B. Eerdmans Publishing Co.

Milligan, G. 1952. *St. Paul's Epistles to the Thessalonians*. Grand Rapids MI: Wm. B. Eerdmans Publishing Co.

Moffatt, J. *The First and Second Epistles of Paul the Apostle to the Thessalonians*. Grand Rapids MI: Wm. B. Eerdmans Publishing Co.

Moore, A. L. 1969. *I and II Thessalonians*. London: Nelson Brothers.

Morris, L. 1957. *The Epistles of Paul to the Thessalonians*. Grand Rapids MI: Wm. B. Eerdmans Publishing Co.

Neil, W. 1950. *The Epistles of Paul to the Thessalonians*. London: Hodder & Stoughton Ltd.

Plummer, A. 1918. *A Commentary on St. Paul's First Epistle to the Thessalonians*. London: R. Scott.

———. 1918. *A Commentary on St. Paul's Second Epistle to the Thessalonians*. London: R. Scott.

Ryrie, C. C. 1959. *First and Second Thessalonians*. Chicago: Moody Press.

Stewart, B. W. 1951. *The Epistles to the Thessalonians*. Aberdeen:

Tatford, F. A. 1953. *The Climax of the Ages*. London: Marshall, Morgan & Scott, Ltd.

———. 1983. *The Final Encounter*. Sydney: Christian Outreach Book Service.

Walvoord, J. F. 1967. *The Thessalonian Epistles*. Grand Rapids MI: Zondervan Publishing Co.

Ward, R. A. 1973. *Commentary on 1 and 2 Thessalonians*. Waco: Word Books.

Whiteley, D. E. H. 1969. *Thessalonians in the R. S. V.* Oxford: Clarendon Press.

Additional Books

Adeney, W. F. Selected texts.

Alexander, W. Selected texts.

Allen, Roland. 1912. *Missionary Methods: St. Paul's or Ours?* London: R. Scott. Reprinted 1956. Chicago: Moody Press.

Anderson, Sir Norman (J. N. D.) 1977. *Issues of Life and Death*. Downers Grove IL: InterVarsity Press.

Barclay, W. 1976. *The Letters of John and Jude*. Philadelphia: Westminster Press.

————. 1959. *The Letters to the Philippians, Colossians, and Thessalonians*. Philadelphia: Westminster Press.

Davidson, A. B. Selected texts.

Dunn, Samuel. 1863. *The Life of Adam Clarke . . . Author of a Commentary on the Old and New Testaments*.

Glasson, T. F. 1945. *The Second Advent*. London: The Epworth Press.

Gloag, P. J. 1888. *Thessalonians I, II—Expositions and Homiletics*.

Lake, K. C. *Contemporary Thinking about Paul*.

Lane, W. L. *Thessalonians*.

Lenski, R. C. H. 1937. *The Interpretation of St. Paul's Epistles to the Colossians, to the Thessalonians, to Timothy, to Titus and to Philemon*. Columbus OH: Lutheran Book Concern.

Lightfoot, J. B. 1893. *Biblical Essays*. London & New York: Macmillan.

———. 1957. *Notes on the Epistles of St. Paul*. Grand Rapids MI: Zondervan.

Manson, T. W. 1962. *Studies in the Gospels and Epistles*. Matthew Black, ed. Philadelphia: Westminster Press.

Mason, A. J. 1883. *The Epistle to the Thessalonians*. London (or "Thessalonians," in *The Handy Commentary*, vol.10. Ellicott, C. J., ed. London: Cassell).

Morton, H. V. 1936. *In the Steps of St. Paul*. London: Reprinted 1948. New York: Dodd, Mead & Co.

Moule, C. F. D. Selected texts.

Moule, H. C. G. (Handley). Selected texts.

Ramsay, Sir Wm. M. 1903. *St. Paul the Traveller and the Roman Citizen*. London: Hodder & Stoughton. Also 1903. New York: G. P. Putnam's.

Robertson, A. T. Selected texts.

Trapp, John. [N. T. Commentary]

Robertson, J. 1893. *The Early Religion of Israel*. Edinburgh: W. Blackwood.

Smeaton, G. 1957. *The Apostles' Doctrine of the Atonement*. Grand Rapids MI: Zondervan. (or 1870. *The Doctrine of the Atonement, as Taught by the Apostles*. Edinburgh: T. & T. Clark).

Swete, H. B. Selected texts.

Warfield, B. B. 1952. *Biblical and Theological Studies*. Samuel G. Craig, ed. Philadelphia: Presbyterian and Reformed Publishing Co.

———. *The Prophecies of St. Paul*.

Young, E. J. 1965–72. *The Book of Isaiah*, Vol. 1. Grand Rapids MI: Wm. B. Eerdmans Publishing Co.